Every Child Is a Genius

Fun and Easy Ways to Develop Your Child's Gifts

Elise M. Griffith

Prima Publishing

Library of Congress Cataloging-in-Publication Data

Griffith, Elise M.
Every child is a genius : 365 fun and easy ways to develop your child's gifts / Elise M. Griffith.
p. cm.
Includes index.
ISBN 0-7615-1277-2
1. Child rearing. 2. Active learning. 3. Education—Parent participation. 4. Family recreation. I. Title.
HQ769.G77 1998
649'.68—dc21

97-52192
CIP

98 99 00 01 BB 10 9 8 7 6 5 4 3 2
Printed in the United States of America

How to Order
Single copies may be ordered from Prima Publishing, P.O. Box 1260BK, Rocklin, CA 95677; telephone (916) 632-4400. Quantity discounts are also available. On your letterhead, include information concerning the intended use of the books and the number of books you wish to purchase.

Visit us online at www.primapublishing.com

This book is proudly dedicated to my mother, Audrey Parker, who inspired a passion for learning that spans two generations, whose love and encouragement gave me the confidence to keep reaching just a little farther, and to whom I owe more thanks than I can ever express.

Contents

Acknowledgments

No individual reaches a goal without the support and encouragement of other people. I'm deeply indebted to my husband, Steven Griffith; thank you for your reassurance, gentle nagging, cheerleading, and most of all for making sure the boys had fun while Mom was busy writing this book. Thanks also to Bobby and Zachary, who keep me young at heart in spite of my graying hair; I'm proud to be your mother. To a miracle baby, Taylor Marie Schmiderer, thank you so much for brightening my days (and long nights) with your precious smile. Thanks also to the friends who listened to my frantic ramblings as I struggled to write this book amidst the chaos of settling into a new home, rounds of the flu, and a million other stresses; you know who you are and you should all be sainted.

I'm forever grateful to the inspirational parents who generously shared favorite activities with me, including: Shawn Armstrong (who contributed to Chapters 1, 2, 3, and 8), Jane Crissman (who contributed to Chapters 2, 3, 6, and 8), Kandie Demarest (for her butterfly experiment, found in Chapter 4), Shari Henry (for her living history activity, found in Chapter 6), Cindy Hudson (for her contributions to Chapters 1, 3, 6, and 8), Mickey Long (for her contributions to Chapter 2), and the many wonderful parents in *Home Education* magazine's forum on America Online who shared their favorite math games with me (Chapter 3). Thanks also go to a talented author, Cynthia Ulrich Tobias, whose dedication to understanding learning styles has helped me become a better parent.

Finally, special thanks to the entire Prima Publishing team—particularly to my editor Susan Silva, who encouraged, developed, and waited patiently for this project to reach its full potential. God bless you all!

Introduction

Today's Fast-Lane Families and the Impact of Busyness on Our Lives

Think about the product name *Day Runner.* What does that name imply? Today's parents are certainly running. On any given day we deal with bills to pay, laundry to wash, bathrooms to scrub, boo-boos to bandage, deadlines to meet, carpools to drive, errands to run, groceries to buy, meals to prepare, and so on. We pencil in doctor's appointments, soccer practices, church or synagogue activities, and school conferences. If we open a newspaper or magazine, we're told that we need to know about mutual funds, political issues, computer technology, and basic nutrition. We worry about increasing college tuition, retirement, the national budget, the dangers lurking on the Internet, and how many fat grams we're consuming.

Statistics show that 75 percent of us live in dual-income families and that we're spending 160 more hours per year at the office than our parents did. We've become so busy that we'll gladly plunk down $20 for a small notebook to help us schedule our days (and nights). What we can't finish one day simply gets added to the next day's long list of things to do. Stress—for many modern parents—has become a way of life. And you know what? We want more time with our children.

According to media reports, our kids need more time with us, too. We worry about them every time we tune in to the 6:00 news or browse through a parenting magazine; we wonder how our children are coping with our tightly scheduled lives. When they look back on their childhoods, what will they remember? How will they fare in the twenty-first century? Will their lives race by faster than our own? Most of all, we wonder if our children will have the necessary skills and confidence to compete in an increasingly competitive world.

What Our Children Need to Succeed in the Twenty-First Century

The American Association of School Administrators conducted a survey to determine the knowledge, skills, and attitudes that grade-school children will need in the coming years. Topping their report was literacy; successful children will have developed a love of language. They'll also understand basic math concepts and will have excellent reasoning and problem-solving skills. Scientific knowledge and applied science will be vital in their education. Computers are here to stay, and successful students will be technologically prepared to access and process information.

According to the report, our children will also need to be well grounded in history and geography. In a world that gets more complicated with every generation, our children deal with issues we couldn't have imagined when we were younger; they'll need to understand a diverse culture. Successful children will also exhibit self-discipline and responsibility and will have a clear sense of what each individual brings to a team. They'll have a healthy respect for themselves and others. Finally, the report states that children in the twenty-first century will need focus, strength of character, morals, and values.

Whew! That's quite a list, isn't it? And that's what schools are for, right? To teach our children all of those things? Well, if you've wandered into a classroom recently, you've probably noticed that, with close to thirty students per teacher, it's impossible for every child to get the kind of attention that's needed to foster all of those necessary skills. Extracurricular activities can help build strength in certain areas, but with strained adult-to-child ratios, some children still slip through the cracks.

At this moment you're probably thinking, "Listen, lady, I have enough trouble keeping household chores at bay; how on earth am I supposed to take on extra duties with everything else I'm juggling?!"

This Book Isn't About . . .

As a woman who juggles too many things too much of the time, I know that guilt is ever-present in my own mind. Therefore, *this book isn't about added guilt.* I'm not going to wag an imaginary finger in your direction with the unspoken message that you're not doing enough, because frankly you're already bombarded with that message everywhere you turn. Television commercials even tell you that! I already feel like I'll never be able to do enough. But I detest guilt, so you're not going to be made to feel guilty as you read this book.

Few of us have enough time to finish reading a magazine article at one sitting—let alone a three-inch-thick reference guide—and we don't want to work too hard to get the information we need. *This book also isn't going to be four hundred pages of everything-you-need-to-know-about-your-child's-curriculum-but-were-afraid-to-ask.* Trust me, there are plenty of those books on the market (I own a few), and I haven't made it past the second chapter with most of them. Therefore, *you're not going to find page-long paragraphs, graduate-school words, or tons of information that you really don't have the energy to wade through.*

Do you sometimes think, if you could just get organized, that you'd accomplish more, strike a better balance between work and home life, and feel better about your life in general? Me, too. And maybe (like me) you have a *Day Runner,* two calendars, organizational software, and color-coded laundry baskets. I always start out with the best of intentions; I practically drool over charts, graphs, and project specification sheets that assure me I'll have a smoother life in just a few short days . . . and I buy them. My motivation always lasts about a week—rarely two. Before long, I discover that I really don't like taking the extra time to write everything down in two or three places and the whole thing fizzles; then I feel guilty.

Since you already know this book isn't about guilt, I'll also let you know that *you aren't going to find any charts, graphs, project specification sheets, or checklists among these pages*. If you're an organized person by nature, you already have those or you know where to find them. If you're less than organized (like me), they aren't going to work for long anyway.

This book also isn't about getting your child to do homework. If homework wars rage in your household, refer to the Resources section at the back of the book; it includes a few titles dedicated to discipline and management tips. My guess, though, is that by the time you've read that far you won't need them.

Finally, *this book isn't about pressuring children to attain lofty educational goals*. I believe that today's children have enough pressures to deal with, and today's parents have more than enough stress. More important, I strongly believe that every child is a genius in one way or another and that—given a few tools, some time, and enough encouragement—any child can reach far beyond our expectations.

So, what *is* this book about? Something completely different than anything you've seen, heard, or read recently: *it's about having fun!*

Bringing Fun Back into Family Life and Education

Do you remember the things you loved to do as a child? Did you ever lose yourself in a rousing game of Scrabble, inventing new words as you went along (and hoping to fake out your opponents)? Did you ever beat the pants off your brother playing Monopoly? Or spend a Saturday afternoon baking cookies with your mother? Do you remember digging in the garden and watching the ants scurry away with larvae? Did you gaze up at the stars on balmy summer nights . . . maybe capturing a firefly or two in a jar? Did your family ever visit out-of-the way places like an old coin shop or spice factory? Perhaps you ventured into a musty museum or collected seashells at the beach? Or maybe one summer you were bored and published a neighborhood newspaper with a few other children?

All of those things were more than fun; they were *educational!* Playing Scrabble strengthened literacy, beating your brother at Monopoly bolstered basic math proficiency, and baking cookies helped develop an aptitude for both math and science. Gardening with a parent opened your eyes and mind to natural science and planted respect for the environment. Stargazing sparked an interest in astronomy and helped take you beyond this earth.

We didn't call them educational—and we certainly didn't think of them that way—but each of those activities reinforced our natural curiosity, creativity, and investigative tendencies. As we played, we built an enduring love for learning that has helped us achieve goals in our adult lives. More than anything else, we were having fun. It was what children did at that time, and perhaps it's what we find missing in our lives today. Think about it: *Are you having fun on a daily basis as a busy parent?* Does the thought of all those wonderful, magical times make you yearn for just a piece of that freedom and excitement again?

Let's face it, today's children don't spend nearly enough time doing the kinds of things we used to enjoy—and neither do we. Organized activities like sports or scouting are great for building character and developing interpersonal skills—and they can even be fun—but our children also need time to play. In fact, even parents need time to play! When your family's calendar is filled months in advance and your ten-year-old asks you for a student *Day Runner*, you can bet that stress is overshadowing enjoyment for everyone.

This book is going to show you how to bring some fun back into your family life, and at the same time help your children do better in school. It's easy. On top of that, as you begin to draw closer together, you'll uncover more time than you knew you had. How? Well, when you relax and forget your worries as you play a round or two of Scrabble—or spend a stress-free weekend exploring your world together—you may start to turn down formerly "essential" activities in favor of family time.

Most of the ideas in this book provide low-cost (or no-cost) fun for everyone. They've been listed according to general subject and include simple, educational experiences for all ages and stages of childhood. It was important that this book be easy to read and use, so you'll notice that each chapter is designed to resemble a collection of four magazine articles. However, you don't need to read the "articles" in sequence. I'd like you to skip around through the chapters and try those activities that appeal to you and your children. *In my mind, this will be a successful book if—after several months—the cover has food stains on it, the binding is badly creased, and the pages are smudged and dog-eared.*

My hope is that by the last page, you'll be gazing at stars and having fun again. All the better when your child brings home a great report card or works on his homework without being scolded.

Some of the tips and ideas may bring back fond memories; others may surprise you. Who knows? As you're reading, you might come up with ideas of your own! If you do, I'd love to hear from you.

I'd also like to know how this book impacts your family life. I'd like to send kudos to your child when his or her grades begin to climb. You can write to me at 2688 Berber Street, Powell, OH 43065.

Together we can build a better future for our children—one family at a time—by bringing fun back into life and learning.

CHAPTER

Beyond Dick and Jane

When September rolls around, just about every magazine on families or parenting features an article geared toward raising a reader. We all want to foster a love of reading because it's the foundation of academic development and success. It's also so much more. Losing yourself in a great book is one of the most rewarding, energizing, liberating, deepening activities around. Better yet, it's cheap! When we read, we embark on adventures and journeys without leaving our comfortable chairs. The written word is a doorway to discovery.

Reading Each Day Helps Keep Boredom at Bay

Do you remember some of your favorite childhood books? Most of us can name a handful. Do you still enjoy a good book today? Or has reading become an activity enjoyed primarily on an airplane or during a day when the weather is foul, the roads are closed, and the cable television stations are unavailable? Carving time in your busy schedule for reading (even if only for half an hour a day) carries benefits beyond entertainment. For example, if you read every day you can:

- Open up to new ideas or remember old concepts long forgotten
- Learn more about yourself, others, and the challenges we all face
- Expand your vocabulary *and* your horizons
- Find creative solutions to everyday stresses and problems
- Possibly lower your blood pressure by distancing yourself from stress for thirty minutes each day
- Give your children one of the most important gifts possible

I hope you caught that last one, because when children see the adults in their lives reading—be it a newspaper, magazine, or book—they usually become strong readers themselves. According to two reputable studies (the first completed by Doris Durkin in 1966, and the second by Denny Taylor and Catherine Dorsey-Gaines in 1988), children who grow up in households where adults are seen reading score higher in reading comprehension than those who don't. In fact, both studies showed that children from every socioeconomic group and IQ range were "early readers" in households where parents enjoyed reading. *In other words, when you take a few minutes out for yourself each day, the whole family benefits.*

Here are some ideas to get you started:

1 Set up a time each day when the adults in the house enjoy literary pursuits—perhaps during the homework hour. Make room in your budget for at least three to six good novels per year and read them.

2 Keep a wide variety of reading materials throughout your home; include a few magazines, a newspaper, and plenty of good books in your selection. Make sure you have material for all ages, including picture books for the tiniest tots.

3 Add a basket or rack of magazines to the most-used bathroom in your home and keep something for everyone there. (One bathroom I visited had copies of *Field & Stream*, *American History*, *Skateboarder*, *Teen Magazine*, and *Ladies' Home Journal*. Obviously, Dad wasn't the only one reading in this bathroom!)

4 Speaking of magazines, consider giving magazine gift subscriptions at the holidays. You'll save yourself a trip to the post office during the holiday rush, and often you won't be billed until the following January. It's

Oprah's Book Club challenges Americans to rediscover great fiction, with astounding results. More than a million women and men have followed her recommendations, uncovered new authors, and pumped life into what had been a sagging industry. If you're having trouble choosing a good novel, peek at Oprah's suggested titles via America Online (keyword: Oprah) or tune in to the show.

one of the simplest, easiest, and most appreciated ways to shop for everyone on your list. Your children will feel special every time an issue arrives in the mail. And while you're at it, why not add a subscription or two to your own "wish list"?

5 Place a few books or articles near your bed for those nights when insomnia threatens. Include things you've been planning to read sometime but haven't gotten around to, like that book on investments and mutual funds. If nothing else, it might put you to sleep.

6 Keep a collection of children's books in a kitchen cabinet. Read one aloud every morning as the children eat their breakfast. If mornings are too chaotic, after-dinner storytime might be just the ticket for family reconnection at the end of a busy day.

7 With the kitchen in mind, what about stashing a few family-oriented magazines within easy reach? That way, when you're out of chicken recipes you can page through a magazine and . . . voilà! And while you're waiting for the oven timer to buzz, you might just make it through that article on affordable family getaways.

8 Most reading materials are transportable, so keep a few paperbacks and children's books in the car for those inevitable delays. You might also try books on tape if your commute is long. Have your children create their own "books on tape": make a recording of each child reading and then replay their stories in the car.

9 Be sure to keep several favorite books in the family room, living room, or den. Inexpensive bookshelves are a good investment, but don't be afraid to leave a few good titles just lying around. You'll be amazed at how often the book on the coffee table is picked up and looked at if you leave it there for a few days.

10 Allow each child to start a collection of books that will be his own. Pick up a small, inexpensive bookshelf to place in his bedroom or closet (plastic shelves are available for as little as $15 on sale), and see how long it takes to fill it up. In fact, you can use books as rewards for good behavior or special achievements.

The Well-Stocked, Well-Organized Family Library on a Budget

It has taken my family thirteen years of slow accumulation to fill seven bookcases in our home. Clearly, we have a wide assortment of reading material, but it's not organized by way of a card catalog—nor do we use the Dewey Decimal system. Like most families, we use a loose organizational system to keep track of which books belong to whom and where they're kept. More on that later in this chapter.

Your first and easiest step to starting your library is to begin stocking it. Keep in mind that you don't have to spend a fortune—unless you have a fortune that you want to spend. There are low-cost and no-cost ways to build a library. Here's a suggested "home library" list for family reading, learning, and entertainment:

- A good selection of colorful children's books—regardless of the ages of your children (at thirty-six, I still love Dr. Seuss)
- At least a handful of the classics, such as *Moby Dick*, *Treasure Island*, *The Adventures of Tom Sawyer*, *Robinson Crusoe*, *The Time Machine*, *Oliver Twist*, *A Tale of Two Cities*, and so on.

- Two up-to-date dictionaries and a thesaurus
- A set of bound encyclopedias (new or used, but in book form)
- A Bible or other religious material that supports your faith and values
- Biographical books of notable figures in history
- Age-appropriate fiction for each family member
- Books that support the special interests in your household
- A few nonfiction titles relating to parenting, family issues, budgeting, etc.
- "Coffee table" or gift books about the arts
- Collections and series books relating to science or history
- Anything FUN!

If you make the effort to buy even three or four books per year, you'll give your children the message that books are important and special. Book clubs help keep the costs down; in most cases, even after paying postage you've saved 20 percent or more off the suggested retail price. Here are some of my favorite sources:

- For a wide selection of affordable children's titles, consider joining

Wal-Mart and other discount stores offer affordable young-reader and youth lines of classic titles under the labels "Great Illustrated Classics" (hardcover) and "Illustrated Classic Editions" (paperback). The paperback versions are small enough—and inexpensive enough—to slip easily into holiday stockings or to tuck under pillows when the Tooth Fairy visits.

Grolier Books, 90 Sherman Turnpike, Danbury, CT 06814–0008.

- Like the adult line, Children's Book-of-the-Month Club offers something for just about any age and interest. For more information, write to them at Children's Book-of-the-Month Club, Camp Hill, PA 17012–0001.
- With titles for the entire family, Great Christian Books might be an appealing club for you. Send your request for club information to: Great Christian Books, 229 South Bridge Street, P.O. Box 8000, Elkton, MD 21922–8000.
- Younger children benefit from Disney's Grow and Learn Library, available at grocery and discount department stores nationwide. Usually a new title is featured each week or month at a price of around $1 (with a minimum general store purchase of $10). A parents' guide is available for each series.
- Contact your local booksellers for independent reading clubs. Border's Books and Music, for exam-

Most of us grew up with *Encyclopedia Britannica,* and now the company offers a wider range of materials to fit just about any budget and situation. For example, *Children's Britannica* is a twenty-volume set with more than 35,000 topics for children ages seven to fourteen. This set is advertised at $250 (new), and can be purchased on a noninterest payment plan by credit card. Call 1-800-372-8264 for more information and a catalog. Be sure to ask about special promotions, sales, and availability of "previous edition" materials.

ple, offers discounts for children who participate in groups and contests sponsored by the store.

- Many elementary schools distribute book club flyers for discounted paperbacks. As a bonus, when you order from the flyer, the school receives free books for classroom use.

While book clubs offer modest savings on purchases, stocking a home library can strain even the most generous budget; if you're like me, you've occasionally struggled with too many bills and too little paycheck. When you're scraping by month to month, books aren't usually a priority purchase. But I have some good news: you can find good-quality books for one-tenth the original cost. You can even get *free* books. It's easier than you might think.

About three years ago, I discovered the thrill of spending Saturday mornings browsing the overflowing shelves at used-book stores. These obscure shops are the best thing around for frugal families. Like their larger, glitzy competitors (national bookstore chains), most offer fresh coffee and a children's reading area. Used-book stores are often nestled in small, out-of-the-way strip malls, so be prepared to drive up and down a few side streets in order to locate the stores listed in your local Yellow Pages. Trust me, though, it's worth the effort. The biggest bonus is that you can trade books you no longer need or want for credit at the store—meaning *free* books for you!

Here's an idea of what you'll find on used-book store shelves:

- Favorite titles from your own childhood
- Slightly out-of-date (but still useful) reference materials—such as dictionaries and encyclopedias

- Paperback novels for as little as $.10 to $.25 each, or hardcover titles for under $5.00

- Cookbooks (including old favorites that are no longer in print)
- Biographies and autobiographies of celebrities and other famous folks
- Gently used and/or slightly out-of-date textbooks
- "Coffee table" and gift books (often in excellent shape)
- Old magazines (and sometimes recent ones for as little as $.25 each)

Once you begin collecting books, you'll discover that accumulation is easy. But organizing your home library can seem intimidating—especially when you have tots, teens, and adults under the same roof. It pays to establish some loose form of organization, and you can use a variety of systems to keep track of your family's books. Keep in mind that small children prefer the dump-them-on-the-floor-and-stand-on-them method of locating a book. When you're a busy parent, the last thing you want to do after tucking the children in at night is assume the role of family librarian—sorting, categorizing, and filing stacks of titles. Here are a few ideas that might make the process easier:

- Designate an area for each child's books (both in the family areas and in the bedrooms). Allow each child to choose a color, then use a permanent marker to color-code the books (example: one child's books carry a red mark on the binding, while another child's books carry a blue mark); at the end of the day, each child is responsible for gathering her own books and putting them away in the designated areas
- You can take color-coding a step farther by using one color to identify the owner and another set of colors to separate

topics, collections, etc. (example: the child with the red mark on the binding also has a gold dot for collections of fiction, a silver dot for storybooks that aren't part of a collection, a green dot for science-related material, a black dot for history or biographies, etc.)

- Sort adult books, reference materials, cookbooks, and so on according to subject on dedicated shelves (example: the upper six shelves in our family room hold my cookbook collection, titles relating to nutritional studies, several "how-to" books arranged by topic, encyclopedias, and religious materials—while the bottom four shelves hold children's books)
- You can, of course, organize fiction in alphabetical order by author, but an easier solution would be to group novels according to genre (example: romance novels on one shelf, science fiction on another, Western or historical titles on a shelf of their own, and so on)
- Sort your books according to priority (example: books you're reading now or plan to read soon on one shelf, along with books the children are currently reading)
- If none of those methods sound organized enough for your temperament, consider computerized labels for a bona fide library-at-home

Tips, Tricks, and Games to Help Teach a Struggling Child to Read

Let's say you already have a lot of reading material in your home, and your child still isn't showing an interest in books. Maybe he's been known to throw a book down and wail, "I can't read this! It's too hard!"

Children struggle with reading for various reasons. Your child might be overwhelmed with stresses unrelated to reading (such as too many extracurricular activities). He might be experiencing a physical problem (such as poor eyesight or problems with hearing speech). Then again, your child may simply fall within the late stage of "normal" reading development. Between the ages of six and nine, most children have grasped the ability to concentrate for long periods of time; to decipher, sort, and categorize symbols; and to express themselves clearly through language (necessary prereading skills).

Of course, in some cases a child is diagnosed with a mild learning disability. If you've been told by the school or your pediatrician that your child has a learning disability (LD), be sure to get another professional's opinion. You'll also want to take your child's unique learning style into account (detailed in Chapter 9). Recent news stories have reported misdiagnosis or "rushed" diagnosis of children who aren't performing at the same level as their peers, although LD isn't necessarily the problem; it doesn't hurt to rule out other possible problems before accepting your child's LD diagnosis.

It's important to understand that a child who's struggling to read often has a corresponding lack of self-esteem. Schools, teachers, and society strongly encourage (and sometimes pressure) children to read early and with good comprehension. Preschoolers are coached in phonics before they're even potty-trained. That's not necessarily a bad thing, but when your daughter's peer group is "better" at reading than she is, she may begin to feel "stupid," and those feelings of humiliation might be the reason for her reluctance to pick up books. If her teacher has called on her to read aloud in front of the class, and she was teased for stumbling over a word, books can become her enemy.

Any time our children struggle, we share their pain and want to help them. There are ways to make reading fun, rather than intimidating. Your participation and positive attitude will speed your child's healing and help her overcome her fears. If at all possible, downplay your own anger, frustration, or concerns. Instead of tutoring your child, *play* with her. The following activities are easy to integrate into your daily routines, they don't cost a lot of money, and they're fun for everyone:

11 Silly songs are an easy way to "teach" spelling and help children learn to identify words. Ever since my sons were small, we've made up songs with familiar tunes, like The Underwear Song:

U-N-D-E-R-W-E-A-R spells underwear
Daddy's in the kitchen in his underwear
Everybody sees him but he doesn't care

The tune doesn't matter, nor does your singing ability. The point is to have fun! More important, you can sing these songs anywhere at any time (although The Underwear Song might not be appropriate in public places with Daddy present).

12 Silly stories are also good for laughs and learning. Have each family member take a turn stating a sentence to make up a story out loud. Each new sentence should start with the next letter of the alphabet. For example, the first person begins: "**A** long time ago, there lived a beautiful princess with purple hair." Then the next person might say: "**B**irds loved this purple hair so much that the princess sometimes found eggs in it." And the next person might say: "**C**an you imagine her surprise when one day an

egg hatched on her head?" The goal (and challenge) is to start the story with the letter A and to end it with a sentence beginning with the letter Z. In most cases, you'll be rolling on the floor with laughter before you're halfway through the alphabet.

13 When you're in the car, make it a point to read signs you pass. If, for example, you pass an antique shop, point out how silly it is that the word is pronounced "an-teek," rather than the way it's spelled: "an-tee-kew." Younger children will almost certainly giggle if you make a game of it. Have everyone join in the search for silly signs.

14 Invent a modified game of charades. Instead of acting out the word, have the players try to guess the word or phrase by drawing the sounds. For example, the word *candy* could be drawn as a can, a plus sign, and the letter D. Once the word has been guessed, write it on the score card next to the name of the family member who guessed it. Set a time limit for guessing and for the game. The player who guesses the most correct words or phrases wins. Because you're using pictures, your child won't feel like he's "reading," but make no mistake—he's learning phonics!

15 Some of the best-loved books are now available as board games. Dr. Seuss' Cat in the Hat (University Games) and Green Eggs and Ham (University Games), while geared for younger children, are fun for the whole family. Each colorful board game teaches reading, rhyming, counting, and memory skills. Besides, who can resist that mischievous cat or Sam I Am?

16 An older child might need a more "grown-up" game, and Scrabble (Milton Bradley) fits into this category. Make sure you have at least one dictionary on the table when you play the game. Instead of playing individually, team up the family so that one adult or older child is paired with your struggling reader. If you have one Scrabble night each week (playing in teams), you should see some improvement within a few months.

17 Televisions manufactured today offer closed captioning. I suggest that you turn this feature on and leave it on. It might seem annoying at first, but within a week or two you'll be used to it. This is an invaluable tool for a child who isn't crazy about books but loves Saturday morning cartoons.

18 Pick up some comic books. It's amazing how often a child will sit with a comic book when one is available. While they're not literary gems, comic books *do* have words (and lots of pictures). And your fourth-grader won't see them as "baby" books. A friend of mine had a reluctant reader who actually developed an interest in books because of the Calvin & Hobbes collections. Superheroes could have the same effect, and it's certainly worth a try.

19 Cookbooks are wonderful for encouraging a reluctant reader; look for colorful ones with plenty of illustrations and easy-to-prepare recipes. Have your child select a recipe or two and compile an ingredient list together. Take your child with you to shop for items you don't have (food labels have words on them, too)—then pull out the cookware and have fun together. Children don't think of cookbooks as "books," so this a nonthreatening way to help your child sound out longer words.

20 Computerized games such as Word Munchers (The Learning Company) can also be a fun, painless way to help your child learn to read. Check out the software sections of your local stores for popular titles, read parenting magazines for software reviews, and check out resale shops for great prices.

21 As crazy as this sounds, a child who is having difficulty reading might benefit from a language program geared to children, such as Berlitz Kids (Universal). For about $30 you can pick up a set of instructional tapes and learn a language together. Why would this help a struggling reader? Because many words in the English language are based on other languages (such as Latin or French), and the novelty of being able to speak in a foreign tongue can get your child past his struggle by bolstering his confidence with language in general.

22 Another unconventional idea involves listening to music from other countries. Children typically love music, embrace anything that's different, and are always enthusiastic about being noisy. Pick up a few cassettes or CDs that have been imported from places like Greece, Turkey, or South America. Soon your children will be singing along at the top of their voices (especially if they know it annoys you). What does this have to do with reading? Literacy is all about language, as I mentioned; a lively musical tempo will help your child grasp the concepts of sequence and organization, which are critical for reading written words.

23 Can an art project help a reluctant reader? You bet! Especially when that project is Word Painting. Begin by making a list of words related to a specific theme or holiday. Keep the words simple (no more than seven or eight letters each, with several that have fewer than six letters), and include no more than ten words on your list. Your child chooses several words from the list you've provided for her and considers which colors of paints, markers, or crayons to use for the project. For example: *rose* could be red, pink, yellow, or peach; she might also choose a color that matches the shape of the object (word), such as orange for the word *circle*. With her words and colors chosen, your child can draw various shapes in a composition, then print the words in the center of each represented color. The resulting artwork should resemble a colorful collage.

2|4 An older child might enjoy making art with a message by choosing a significant phrase (such as: "A good book is the best of friends, the same today as forever."—Martin Tupper), and then creating a poster that repeats the message several times using cut paper, paint, or ink. The words themselves become your child's artistic expression, and the chosen phrase is the main element of his work.

If, after trying several fun activities, your child continues to have difficulty with reading, her doctor or teacher may suggest that you purchase a phonics program. Try to review the material before you buy it because many phonics programs are dull and boring. Look for materials that are colorful or enticing, and try to find something that appeals to your child's tastes and interests. GCB offers a product called Phonogram Fun Packet (from Beall's Learning Games), which is an enjoyable alternative to more "scholastic" phonics kits. For more information about the Phonogram Fun Packet, call GCB at 1-800-775-5422.

Literary Adventures the Whole Family Will Love

Books can take you far beyond the printed page; you'd be amazed at how often an adventure can be sparked in the aisles of a public library. Even the most unlikely title could open a treasure chest of experiences for your family to share together, and it's the best way to instill a lifelong love of reading and learning. How? Often accidentally during foul weather. I'll share an experience to illustrate what I mean.

A few years ago, I came across a Winnie-the-Pooh cookbook while at the public library. In it, there were some wonderful recipes for teatime treats. This gave me an idea: we planned a tea party! I checked out the book (along with a few other books about tea and tea parties), and the next time the skies were gray we baked honey cakes, brewed herb tea, pulled out the china, and dressed up. Our tea party was a smashing success (fortunately, none of the china was smashed in the process). As we sipped and gobbled, we discussed various types of tea, where they're harvested, where and when tea parties originated, how to brew a proper pot of tea, and more.

It just so happened that we lived near Boulder, Colorado, at that time—home to the Celestial Seasonings tea company. The following Saturday morning, we headed north for a tour. In other words, one simple children's cookbook provided us with two weeks of adventures and a rich education that included science, history, sociology, and economics. Christopher Robin would have been proud!

Any book can unfold into a fun learning experience for your whole family. It's easier than you think to pull ideas from the pages of a book, and once your creative juices begin to flow, you'll rarely lack weekend entertainment. Here are some suggestions to get you started:

25 There is something significant about each geographic area of the United States. Next time you're at the public library, pick up a children's book about your state. Learn about the state's history, geography, and so forth. Involve the family in making a state flag. Plant the state flower in your yard (or in a pot on your patio). Check with the Chamber of Commerce to find out about important landmarks, museums, tours, and events in your area. You should be able to pull at least a month's worth of weekend adventures from this information.

26 Have your children pick out a few books about nature, the environment, birds or bird-watching, and similar topics. Watch to see what sparks each child's interest and play off that. A National Park is an obvious starting point for family fun. Provide each family member with a small notebook and see how many different types of plants and animals you can identify. Walk the nature trails, enjoy a picnic, and be sure to take some photographs. After your day at the park, contact the local disposal company to find out about the recycling centers in your area. Arrange for a tour of the facilities. Pick up brochures or information about recycling and composting, and begin your own family recycling project. Build a bird feeder. Plant a garden of native shrubs and flowers (such as those your children noticed during your park visit).

27 A book about sports can provide a season's worth of learning—whether it's basketball, baseball, or football, you'll have plenty of opportunities for fun. High school sporting events provide low-cost entertainment, and don't forget the local minor leagues or college games. Incorporate a study of the history of the game. When and where did it become a recognized sport? Who were the players on the first big teams? Your children might enjoy keeping stats, collecting cards, and writing letters to their favorite teams or sports celebrities.

28 If your child shows an interest in coins and currency, check with the library for a book about coin collecting. You should be able to find an old coin shop in your area. Help your child start a collection of his own. You can also make edible pennies on a drizzly Saturday afternoon by purchasing and preparing a box of gingerbread mix, rolling the dough, cutting the dough into small circles, and gently pressing a design into the surface of each (using a clean toy or a store-bought mold) before baking them.

29 Our oldest son was into the Hardy Boys mystery series for a while; you can come up with fun adventures from this type of book as well. Instead of focusing on the main characters, focus on the location, theme, events, or main points of the story. For example: if the story takes place near a seashore, you might spend an afternoon building a lighthouse or a boat out of craft wood. Serve dinner by candlelight; be sure fish is included in the main entree. If you live near a large body of water, plan a weekend excursion to the shore.

30 Many children (girls and boys alike) love horses. Pick up a copy of *Black Beauty* the next time you're at the public library or a bookstore and read it together as a family. If you live in or near a rural area, see if you can visit a farm that has horses. City dwellers might enjoy a Saturday at the racetrack. Spend a day at the next rodeo that comes to town. Read about various breeds of horses and begin a collection of horse figurines. Hold a Ranch Party: serve classic ranch-style food and your ask your guests to wear Western clothing.

31 The classic *Jungle Book* (or the children's tamer version) forms the basis for any number of adventures. Begin with a trip to the local zoo and be sure to spend time at the bear, orangutan, panther, tiger, and wolf exhibits. Host a safari for neighborhood children (similar to an Easter Egg hunt, but hide smaller trinkets all over your home or yard). Embark on a mini-study of India, then visit an authentic Indian restaurant. Enjoy an afternoon matinee watching the movie versions of the book (including all the versions you can find at your local video shop). Have your children compare and critique the videos against the original novel.

32 When I was in school, a book sparked my interest in Father Junipero Serra and the missions he founded along the Pacific coast (we lived in central California). It took more than a year of occasional weekend trips, but my family eventually visited each one. We learned a lot about the Catholic Church, California history, and the lore surrounding each mission—such as the return of the swallows to the Mission at San Juan Capistrano every year. Families in Kentucky, Ohio, and Pennsylvania might want to travel along the route of the Underground Railroad, beginning with a book about Harriet Tubman.

33 Check out some library books with stories about the circus and get ready for popcorn and peanuts the next time one rolls into town. Study the history of the traveling circus, or simply study the history of clowns (beginning with court jesters). Review the differences between a carnival and a circus. Or put on your own three-ring show!

Do you see what I mean? Books pique and enhance a child's interest in the world around her. They can also act as a springboard for some wonderful, memorable day trips and adventures. Best of all, they open doors to new experiences and learning opportunities for everyone. Why not see where they take your family?

CHAPTER

Pencil It In

Have you ever experienced something so moving—so extraordinary—that you found yourself at a loss for words to adequately express your emotions? Or struggled with a problem so complex that you weren't sure you could define it?

We live in a world that depends on words, yet true literacy involves more than the ability to read; it begs us to explore a deeper understanding of how and why we use language as the ultimate expression of ourselves. From the moment we're born, we learn to communicate with the people around us by cooing, smiling, or crying. Have you ever wished a wailing infant would just pipe up and say, "Mom! Burp me please, I have a tummy ache!" Cooing gives way to babbling, which is followed by single words and two-word sentences, such as "Baba mik!" Eventually a child adds more words that open pathways to understanding; a three- or four-year-old will specify what *kind* of milk (cold, chocolate, etc.) and even which cup he prefers to drink from. As he masters verbal skills, he begins to understand that language plays a critical role in his ability to express his needs, wants, and feelings.

Putting a Child's Thoughts on Paper

Writing is the fulfillment (or maturity) of speech, and helps us more clearly express what we want to say. Talking is one form of organized thought, and written speech is a deeper, more deliberate way to structure what we're trying to chronicle or communicate. For example, as I write this book I must consider you—the reader—and find a way to express encouragement, support, and perhaps even a smile or two as I present information that I hope will be useful for your family. How could I do that if we were talking on the telephone? Chances are I'd fail in one area or another, either by coming off as a busybody and know-it-all, or by leaving out important points along the way.

> *"Words, like eyeglasses, blur everything that they do not make clear."*
>
> —JOSEPH JOUBERT

The ability to write is one of the most critical skills our children need for a successful future. Let's explore a few time-honored ways to build your child's writing skills, beginning not with your children, but with *you*. The following activities will help you rediscover your daydreams, record your deepest feelings, put plans to paper, or simply keep in touch with your friends and family.

34 Write letters to yourself every now and then. Buy special stationery. Fill yourself in on your life, family, job, and activities. Discuss your goals, dreams, disappointments, and prospects. When your children ask you who you're writing to, tell them! Who knows? They might worry a little and pitch in more with the housework.

35 Speed-dialing is faster (and more convenient) than the post office, but you can cut your phone bill by writing letters to distant friends and family. E-mail might be tempting, but pull out that special stationery again. Have your children enclose notes of their own to accompany your letters. Grandparents, aunts, and uncles love getting letters from children. You don't have to write seven-page sonnets; start with a page or two, including the children's notes.

36 Start a photo journal. Dust off your camera, pick up packages of fresh batteries and film, and record your experiences for an entire day. Example: I used to work thirty-five minutes from home at a small art-supply store on the edge of town. One day, I brought my Polaroid camera and snapped photographs of various things when the traffic slowed to a crawl. Later that day, I took pictures of the view through the front windows of the shop. When I made a quick run to the bank in the early afternoon, I captured a photograph of water rushing under a nearby bridge. I finished off the film at home, photographing the boys at play. It was clear that simple pleasures were the moments I'd been compelled to capture. I realized my job and commute left little time to fully enjoy those things, so I scaled back my hours. Within a few months I gave notice and revived my

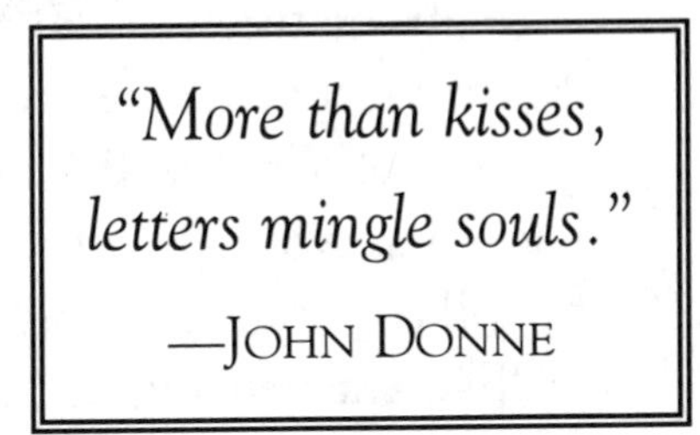
"More than kisses, letters mingle souls."

—John Donne

home-based business. The moments you photograph can reveal hidden needs or desires.

37 Clip pictures from magazines or catalogs that illustrate your goals and dreams, then paste them in a special scrapbook. Jack Canfield and Mark Victor Hanson, authors of the *Chicken Soup for the Soul* series, theorize that keeping this kind of scrapbook sparks one's subconscious creativity. They believe that a tactile project (like creating such a scrapbook) leads to recognizing subtle opportunities that can make your dreams realities. Besides, it's fun!

38 If you love to putter among the flowers, start a gardener's journal. You don't need anything fancy for this; a simple spiral notebook will do. Periodically jot down ideas for potted plants or formal beds, and sketch or paste in pictures of favorite species. Dreary winter days are the best time for this sort of activity. Be sure to include notations about your preferred colors, the soil requirements, and similar criteria. Even if you live in an apartment complex with a teensy patio or balcony, you can still plan a container garden—or a future landscape.

Scrapbooks are making a comeback. Entire aisles of stores are devoted to scrapbook materials; there are even some companies that offer home parties devoted to organizing family mementos, locks of baby hair, special achievements, and so on. Scrapbook prices range from $5 to $50 or more, depending on the type of pages (acid-free paper costs more).

39 Maybe you have a gray thumb but golden fingers and prefer

crafts to flower beds? Keep a craft diary, listing ideas for projects, gifts, and decorations. Next time you're at the flea market, or you spot something you adore in a gift shop, record it in your craft diary. A benefit to this is that when you need a quick gift, you'll have pages of ideas to pull from.

40 Start a special journal for each of your children. Purchase a blank book and periodically record their interests, developments, successes, and struggles. Include your own thoughts and feelings as a parent. I began writing in each of my boys' journals weekly, but by the time they were toddling, I dropped down to monthly entries. Now I write a handful of pages each year. I have no idea if I'll ever get those journals filled, but I do know that each boy will take a nugget of his childhood with him when he leaves home.

41 A spiritual diary is a place to record your deepest self, conversations with God, meaningful passages, and pressing concerns. Becky Tirabassi offers a product called *The Prayer Partner Notebook*, which is available at Christian bookstores nationwide. Like a traditional notebook, it contains sections and dividers for each topic covered in her accompanying book, *Let Prayer Change Your Life*. If you celebrate a different faith, you can adapt her idea to fit your needs and beliefs. Buy a three-ring binder, notebook paper, and a package of dividers (you might want to purchase dividers with pockets to hold special poems, greeting cards, and other loose items). Categorize the spiritual elements in your life, and use those categories as the sections in your journal.

I hope one or two of these ideas sparked your interest. Some of them can be modified for teenagers and young adults. What about younger children? How can you encourage your child to put her thoughts on paper? Journaling is an obvious choice, but the key to success is expanding her boundaries of self-expression to include more than "Dear Diary." Here are a few unconventional examples, listed by age level:

Preschool Through Second Grade

Just as primitive writing was made up of hieroglyphics, a child's first attempts at written expression usually come in the form of pictures, symbols, and objects.

42 Preschoolers and kindergartners haven't yet mastered the skills to write about their experiences, interests, concerns, or feelings, but they sure love to paint! Keep watercolor paper, inexpensive brushes, and nontoxic paints on hand for spontaneous fun. You'll also want some plastic or foam cups; paper towels or rags; an old, adult-sized shirt (as a smock); and a vinyl tablecloth. Have your child help you set up a still-life scene using favorite objects from around the house and be sure to include fresh flowers if they're available. Pull out the paper, brushes, and paints. The items your child chooses to paint, and the colors he picks, will give you an idea about what he's feeling.

43 Beginners benefit from keeping a journal box. Small children can store cherished items in a special container that you create from an old shoe box, cigar box, baby-wipe box, or other

container that has a lid. Spray-paint it, cover it with fabric or colorful paper, and glue on buttons, "jewels," or anything else to make it unique and fancy-looking. Present it with fanfare, and tell your child that his journal box is for storing his most prized trinkets. Assure him that no one else will ever touch it without his permission, and make sure siblings understand that they're not allowed to violate his privacy.

44 Scrapbooks or photo albums made by and for each child are really pictorial diaries. In essence, the child is recreating the world she sees. Newspaper clippings, postcards, letters, gum wrappers, Polaroid pictures, drawings, poems—just about anything—can become important enough to grace the pages. A basic, inexpensive scrapbook will run about $5 to $10 at a discount store, and you can get a plastic-sleeved photo album for as little as $2.

45 Seven-year-olds love cartoons and comic strips, and this is often the age when they begin to wonder how the characters are made. Craft and art supply stores carry a wide range of books, videos, and complete kits on cartooning. Some stores, such as the Dick Blick Art Materials chain, rent instructional videos for a small fee. What does cartooning have to do with journaling? Everything! Your gradeschooler might balk at the idea of writing in a diary, yet love the idea of developing his own comic strip. And here's a little secret: the characters and

Working with watercolors and paintbrushes helps develop the fine motor skills necessary for good penmanship—in fact, if your kindergartner is struggling with a pencil, let her use paint when she's practicing her letters.

story lines your child develops will run parallel with his experiences, daydreams, and fears.

Third Through Fifth Grade

As your child's writing skills begin to mature, encourage special-interest journaling.

46 A Weather Journal is ideal for the child who's fascinated with gardening and/or natural sciences. You'll need a three-ring binder, notebook paper, graph paper, an assortment of colored pencils or markers, and access to weather reports (the 5:00 news or cable weather channels work well). Have your child record weather predictions and compare them to actual conditions. The graph paper enables her to chart weather patterns and seasonal changes; the lined notebook paper provides ample space for her to record her own observations and questions.

47 Friendship Journals are popular with elementary school children. Purchase a plain sketchbook (these cost anywhere from $10 to $15, depending on the size) and a handful of paint pens (about $2 each) so that the cover can be decorated and customized. Along with your child's own thoughts and musings, the Friendship Journal is passed around through his group of friends. The concept is similar to a high-school yearbook; each friend writes a message to your child and signs his or her name. Photographs of the friends can be pasted on the entry pages, and your child can add notes about activities enjoyed with this person after the entry. In a year or two, the friendship journal will be filled with happy memories.

48 If your child loves books, try a Reading Journal, which is an expanded version of the journals kept in classrooms and school libraries. A simple spiral notebook works well. Instead of simply recording title, author, and date, your child records her thoughts about the characters, story line, and other aspects of the story. She can also put herself in the place of the main characters and "rewrite" sections of books to fit her life and environment. If she aspires to the life of a writer, she might critique the authors or make notes about an author's life and interests (bookstores and libraries can help her find this information).

> *"A writer must write what he has to say, not speak it."*
>
> —Ernest Hemingway

49 Perhaps your son is a sports nut. A Sports Journal gives him the opportunity to follow teams and players, record stats, jot down his thoughts about each game, and organize collector cards. He'll need a three-ring binder, notebook paper, tabbed dividers (one for each team or sport), and a package of pocketed vinyl photo-album sheets that fit into the journal; zippered vinyl accessory pouches hold colored pens, ticket stubs, and autographs. A true sports enthusiast doesn't need any instruction for keeping a Sports Journal; he'll probably ask for a new one each season!

50 An Image Journal utilizes writing and drawings or pictures to convey a child's feelings, impressions, and ideas. The best way to keep an Image Journal is by using a scrapbook, rather than a notebook. The scrapbook should be large enough to hold photographs, magazine clippings, postcards, and similar items, yet small enough to fit into a backpack. Your child collects "images," pastes them in her journal, and records her thoughts about them.

She can also use her chosen "images" as illustration for ideas, jotting down her plans in the blank spaces on the page.

Sixth Through Eighth Grade

Adolescent children face confusing emotions and issues every day. Preteens and young teens also tend to withdraw from their parents during this phase, but they need an outlet to make sense of it all—journaling is an excellent way to do just that.

51 My Life, Rewritten is a special kind of journal, ideally suited to junior-high-aged children. They're at that awkward, in-between stage—not a child and not quite a teen. Their peers can be unbelievably cruel. Everything embarrasses an adolescent. My Life, Rewritten can be recorded in a traditional blank journal or on the computer. In this journal, your preteen safely records upsetting, confusing, or embarrassing moments of the day, but rewrites them with a happier ending. In other words, rather than writing about the boy on the bus who pulled up her skirt and flashed her bikini panties to everyone behind her—or mentioning the boy who yelled from the back of the bus, "Hey! Boulder Butt!"—your daughter rewrites the script any way she wants. If she actually burst into tears (further embarrassing herself), she might fictionalize it so that she, instead, turns the tables on her antagonizer. Or she may decide to write the story as if she'd been able to avoid the entire fiasco by catching a ride home with a popular classmate. Whatever way she chooses to rewrite her life story, privacy must be respected; if she's keeping her journal on the computer, make sure her files can't be accessed by anyone else in the family.

52 A Gratitude Journal provides a way to focus on some of the positive aspects of your preteen's life. Any junior-high-aged child can write pages of negatives about his life: his parents are unreasonable and just don't understand, his friends are critical, his teachers hate him, the girl he secretly idolizes has no idea he's alive, and he never gets picked for sports teams. At this age, it's easy to overlook the good that's there along with the bad. In order to encourage a Gratitude Journal, start by using it as a family activity. Have each member of the family list one thing each day for which he or she is grateful. Instead of writing them in a journal, write them on scraps of paper and have everyone try to guess who wrote each one. Yes, your preteen with think this is a lame exercise at first, but in time he'll warm up to the idea. That's when you buy him a journal of his own and encourage him to record bright spots in his day, things he's thankful for, or people who have been kind to him.

> *"Writing is no trouble: you just jot down ideas that occur to you. The jotting is simplicity in itself—it is the occurring which is difficult."*
>
> —STEPHEN LEACOCK

53 My Favorite Things Journal adds an affirming element to an otherwise perplexing phase of life. Favorite things go beyond what your child is grateful for to encompass all that's special, meaningful, or intriguing. She'll need a good-sized scrapbook and a small box or container. Combining elements of the Gratitude Journal and the Image Journal, My Favorite Things Journal holds clippings, photographs, letters, and pictures, with notations about each. Items that are too large or bulky to paste onto the pages of the scrapbook can rest safely in the box. Again, this is a very personal activity; your child's privacy should be carefully guarded.

Organized Thought Grows from Fun Family Writing Games

Journaling is a solitary activity that enhances your child's ability to structure his or her thoughts. Fun activities for the whole family can further build on those skills. Young children can partner with an adult who helps them write (or who writes for them). To get started, you'll need paper, pencils or pens, and a lively sense of humor. Some of the following games require additional materials, but all of them are guaranteed to get your gang giggling, thinking, and writing.

54 That's a Lulu is a family game developed by Luella Bouchard in New Paltz, New York. Designed during a holiday gathering, this game becomes more hilarious with a large number of players. It's based around a number of interesting, thought-provoking, and sometimes silly questions. Each player writes his or her answers to the posed questions anonymously, and everyone tries to match responses to players. The entire game (including question cards and score sheets) comes in a small, water-resistant, zippered pouch that fits easily into a purse, knapsack, or diaper bag. Luella is now in the process of developing a children's version that will be available (along with her original game) in gift shops and specialty stores. For more information, write to: That's a Lulu, 16 Apple Road, New Paltz, NY 12561, or e-mail AJB66@juno.com.

55 Mystery Messages requires "color change" felt-tipped markers (available from Crayola), white 3-by-5-inch cards, a pair of dice, and at least three players. Start by rolling the dice to determine the villain of the first round (the person who rolls the highest number becomes the villain). The villain has a few minutes to secretly choose an object within view and (using a Crayola colorless marker) write one clue on each of the 12 3-by-5-inch cards. For example, some clues might hint at physical aspects the object has, such as: Margaret likes blue balloons, but I prefer red. Others might suggest a location, such as: Have you read a good book lately? Each remaining player rolls one of the dice to determine how many clue cards he or she will receive. For example, if a player rolls a three, then three cards are picked up. Players continue to roll until all of the clue cards have been distributed. If, by some chance, there is a player without a clue card, he can "challenge" another player by rolling one of the dice; if the number is equal to or less than the number of clue cards the challengee is holding, it's considered a "fair" challenge. The challengee then rolls one of the dice, and if her number is higher than the challenger's, she keeps all of her clue cards; if the number is lower, she must give one clue card to the challenger. If the challenger loses, he may challenge another player and continue to challenge players until he wins a clue card. When every player has at least one clue card, they take turns revealing their invisible ink clues by coloring over the clear ink with one of the other markers in the package. Players are allowed to use all of the clues to solve the mystery. The first player to correctly solve the mystery wins—and becomes the villain in the next round.

56 Another fun mystery game is Who Am I? You'll need two sheets of paper and a pencil for each player. Everyone is instructed to choose a sports star, politician, television personality, or other famous person. They write the name of that person on one piece of paper and fold the paper in half twice (to be sure the written name can't be seen through the folds). Each player then puts his or her own name on the outside flap of the folded paper, and the folded slips of paper are piled in the middle of the playing table.

One at a time, players draw a folded slip of paper. If a player draws her own, she must put it back in the pile or trade with someone else. When everyone has a "playing piece," they take turns asking questions and recording the answers on their other sheet of paper (without opening the folded sheet). Questions are posed to the person whose name is on the outside flap. For example, a player might ask the person who chose Magic Johnson, "Is your person male or female?" and would write the answer "male" on the answer sheet. Each player is allowed to ask one question per turn, with a total limit of ten questions. Anyone who guesses the answer to "Who Am I?" in ten questions or less wins the game. At the end of the game, each piece of paper is opened and all names are revealed.

57 A quick game with funny results is Family Shorts. The object of the game is to compose a short story by putting together individual sentences. Taking turns, each player finishes a part of a story by writing it on a piece of paper. Everyone keeps their responses to themselves until all parts of the story have been written. You can use the following format or come up with a basic story line of your own: "Once upon a time [girl's name] . . . went to the [place] . . . to visit [boy's name]. . . . She told him she had been [activity]. . . . He said [phrase] . . . so they decided to [activity]. The end." Cards containing each segment are distributed evenly and each player fills in the blank(s) for his card(s). Then all cards are put together to complete the story. The total number of sentences should be six to eight. Keep it simple, requiring only names, activities, places, and phrases to fill out your family's short story. This is a great way to talk about the definition of nouns, verbs, adjectives, and adverbs. It also helps to boost creative writing skills. Your children will enjoy discovering new story lines each time they play.

From Neighborhood Newspapers to National Magazines

When your children have developed a habit of regularly writing in a journal or enjoying family writing games, you may wind up with a budding author. There is a saying that's tossed around in writer's groups: You don't choose writing; writing chooses you. A child with a passion to pen his thoughts should be celebrated, and that little darling who asks dozens of questions might someday become a sought-after journalist.

During a humid summer in Virginia almost twenty-six years ago, a group of bored grade-schoolers decided to publish a neighborhood newspaper. Armed with notebooks and pens, these dedicated children combed the streets for interesting stories and breaking news. They gathered material, typed it up (making carbon copies), and circulated the first issue. Then they decided to type columns, cut and paste them into a format that resembled a smaller version of the city's newspaper, and mimeograph future issues. Unfortunately, there didn't seem to be enough hot gossip to maintain interest, and soon many of the staff were back to playing kickball. Yet two writers were born that summer; I'm one of them.

Your children can not only learn to write, type, edit, format, print, and distribute a neighborhood newspaper; they can publish short stories, poetry, magazine articles, plays, and even songs. All they need is some encouragement and a bit of help from you. Here are some ideas to get you started:

58 If you subscribe to a daily newspaper, your preschooler has probably watched you page through the morning edition—and may even pretend to read the paper herself at times. You can make this time together special with a little fanfare when your paper runs a children's section: sprawl out together and spread the newspaper on the floor (presenting her with her very own section). If she's able to count, point out the number of pages and the amount of writing on them. Show her the articles and drawings that were submitted by children. Make this a semiregular ritual and, by the time she learns to write, you may have a special clipping to send to family and friends—with your child's byline!

59 Expand that encouragement by presenting your five- or six-year-old with a used typewriter, typing paper, a children's dictionary, and an "editor's" visor. Kindergartners and first graders love to pretend; he'll enjoy hours of make-believe as he "interviews" family members and "publishes" his newspaper.

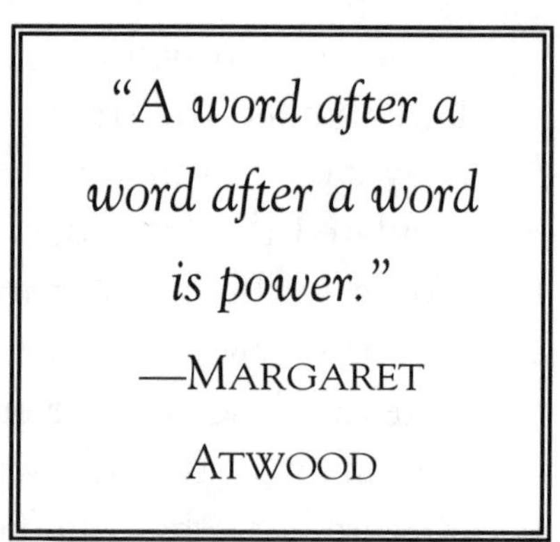

60 Your second-grader should have enough verbal skills to open the presses for a small children's newspaper or newsletter, and she can distribute each issue to her friends and classmates. She can write, type, or computerize general articles, entertainment reviews (books, television shows, movies, etc.), recipes, and advertisements. Let her study your local newspaper to get ideas about what kinds of things she'd like to cover, and encourage her to enlist the help of "stringers" (children who will attend events, read a book, or watch a movie and report on it). Simply take the "galleys" (original copies) to a print shop and run inexpensive copies for her.

61 An eight- to ten-year-old might want to consider publishing a helpful newspaper for area newcomers, called

Welcome to the Neighborhood; this publication should include the names, addresses, and telephone numbers of local businesses, churches, schools, doctors, and services, as well as a listing of neighborhood baby-sitters, housekeepers, and lawn-mowing enterprises (run by children and teens). The paper can also highlight special events, upcoming craft shows, school programs, and more. If your child approaches local businesses with a sample copy of the paper, he can sell enough advertising space to cover the cost of printing and distribution; most small business owners will happily purchase low-cost ad space to help out an enterprising young publisher.

62 Buy your young writer a copy of *Young Author's Guide to Publishers* and read it together. She'll find out how to become a serious writer, what research markets are open to children, how to submit query letters and manuscripts to editors, or how to enter contests. At $8.95, this book is a bargain that can

Raspberry Publications, Inc., is a children's book publisher with works by children and for children—ranging from picture books to young adult fiction and nonfiction. Always looking for fresh talent, they've launched a new line of junior novels called "The Raspberry Crime Files." Beginning with their first child author (who is the niece of one of the publishers), the company hopes to inspire other talented young people, to encourage small presses. They accept submissions year-round and are one of the few publishers who will accept handwritten manuscripts. Raspberry books are sold nationally through several reputable bookstore chains.

launch your child's career! Ask your local bookseller to order the book if you don't see it in the store, or write to Raspberry Publications, Inc., P.O. Box 925, Westerville, OH 43086.

63 You can encourage your child to follow in the footsteps of young magazine mogul Cecelia Schmitt, a homeschooled twelve-year-old who publishes *Creature Feature*. Cecelia's magazine includes stories, articles, poems, book and movie reviews, animal advice, columns, and quizzes for readers ranging in age from preschool to retirement. Your child can create a magazine that focuses on a specific or general topic with the help of a software package such as PageMaker (Adobe) or Page Plus (Serif), a friendly print shop, and a bulk mailing account with the post office. The publishing software will allow him to lay out articles, artwork, and advertisements. Any word-processing program can perform basic editing with spell-check and grammar-check tools. This is a fabulous activity to share with your child, and the educational benefits are limitless.

64 If publishing her own magazine seems too time-consuming, your child might prefer to do some freelance writing for children's magazines. Take her to a bookstore and have her page through magazines that interest her. If she finds a handful that she thinks she'd like to write for, purchase them and suggest that she not only read the articles but also study the ads carefully; ads tell you a lot about the readers' interests. Next comes a trip to the library; your child will need to review back issues to make sure that her story (or something similar) hasn't been published in the past several months. If not, help her draft a basic outline to organize her thoughts. She should write a first draft, then put it aside for at least one day. When she reviews it, she'll be able to find any errors. Help her check the spelling, grammar, and punctuation before she writes her final draft. She should edit her material again before submitting the work to the magazine. Always include a self-addressed stamped envelope for the return of her manuscript.

Here are a few of the most popular children's magazines that use material submitted by children (available wherever magazines are sold):

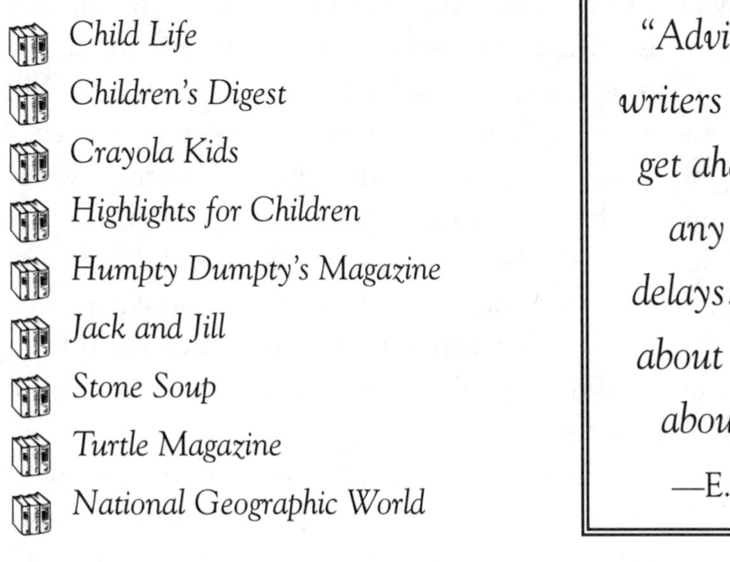

- *Child Life*
- *Children's Digest*
- *Crayola Kids*
- *Highlights for Children*
- *Humpty Dumpty's Magazine*
- *Jack and Jill*
- *Stone Soup*
- *Turtle Magazine*
- *National Geographic World*

> *"Advice to young writers who want to get ahead without any annoying delays: don't write about Man, write about a man."*
>
> —E. B. WHITE

65 Any teen with a talent for storytelling will want to enter *Aim Magazine*'s Short Story Contest. There is no fee to enter, but all entries must be received by August 15th every calendar year. The focus of your teen's short story should encourage racial/ethnic acceptance (without a preachy tone). Send submissions to Aim Magazine Short Story Contest, P.O. Box 20554, Chicago, IL 60620.

66 Younger children can submit poems or short stories for consideration in *Cricket* magazine's annual contest. For contest rules and deadlines, write to Cricket League Contests, P.O. Box 300, Peru, IL 61354; be sure to include a self-addressed stamped envelope.

Family Publishing for Fun and Profit

As I write this book, the weather forecast indicates that snow is on the way to my area of the country—and that means Christmas is gaining on this busy Mom! Every harried parent shivers at the thought of approaching holidays, and it's not because there's a chill in the air. How will we juggle the demands of work, family, cleaning, shopping, wrapping, mailing, baking, and decorating, while keeping jolly smiles plastered across our tired faces? Perhaps the most daunting aspect of the holiday season is finding the time and money to buy gifts for everyone on our Christmas/Hanukkah lists. And if you're like me, you have friends and family scattered from coast to coast, meaning that you're also going to drop a chunk of change to mail those gifts.

What if I told you there was an easier way? What if you could gather your children and make quick, inexpensive holiday cards and gifts that can be shipped for a fraction of what it costs to mail that slicer-dicer kitchen gizmo or the his-and-hers lime-and-purple sweaters? What if the gifts you send this year could last longer than that mail-ordered box of salami and cheese—or the perfume that gives Aunt Nancy a migraine?

You don't need a great deal of time or writing skill to create winning greeting cards, cookbooks, "how-to" books, collections of poetry, annual newsletters, picture books, stationery sets, or other family publishing projects. You may have so much fun that you decide to sell your creations to the general public! Consider these ideas:

67 Purchase a few boxes of blank greeting cards (available at stationery, craft, and art supply stores nationwide), and for less than $15 you can send personalized greetings to everyone on your mailing list this holiday season. Gather the entire family at the kitchen table; pass out paints, markers, stickers, stamp pads, crayons, glue, bits of felt, "jewels," or any other material; and spend one evening making mini-masterpieces. Allow your children to write the inside greeting (small children can dictate to an older child or adult), and encourage everyone to sign each card.

68 Do you have some family recipes that are child-tested and approved? Buy a package of blank 3-by-5-inch cards, and create recipe cards that your children can slip into photo-sleeves of purchased clear vinyl notebook sheets. Purchase full-page vinyl page protectors, and let your children illustrate on standard typing paper the "chapter page" for each cookbook section. Finally, pass out permanent markers, paint pens, or poster paints and have your children decorate canvas three-ring binders to act as the book jackets. Then assemble the cookbooks together. This project will take about three evenings of fun from start to finish.

69 Heloise isn't the only one who has unique tips for running a busy (and messy) household. I'll bet your family could come up with an entire "how-to-do-it-better" guide; just ask your children! Buy one blank journal and one package of notebook tabs for each child, then assign the following categories: kitchen tips, cleaning tips, yard tips, recycling tips, parenting tips, and kid tips. Help your children attach six tabs (equally spaced) throughout the blank journal, and ask each child to write—or dictate—his ideas for better ways to do things under each category. Some of the ideas might actually be useful but, if nothing else, this will make a good

comic book for special family members (grandparents especially enjoy sharing these during bridge club).

70 Is there a poet in your house? Adolescents often dabble in poetry during this period in their lives, and they can write a collection of poems for holiday gift-giving. Again, it costs little more than $5 for a blank journal. I recommend that you also spend a few dollars for a special ink pen—preferably a fountain pen, which seems to encourage sophisticated literary prowess. If your preteen is especially proud of one or two poems, consider submitting them to a poetry contest, such as the Louise Louis/Emily F. Bourne Student Poetry Contest, Poetry Society of America, 15 Gramercy Park, New York, NY 10003. Be sure to mail the entry before December 22nd of any calendar year.

71 Perhaps your four- or five-year-old shows artistic talent. Why not let her write and illustrate a book of her own this holiday season? It's easier than you might think! Teachers' supply stores (such as Teacher's Helper) and art materials stores (such as Dick Blick Art Materials) sell inexpensive, white-cover, bound blank books that are the same size as most children's books. The covers and pages are made with fade-resistant white paper that accepts any crayons or markers. Buy one for each child, and toss in a package of new water-based markers. For a total cost of about $10 your child will have several hours of fun and a book of her very own. If she enjoys this activity, ask her to make a storybook for each set of grandpar-

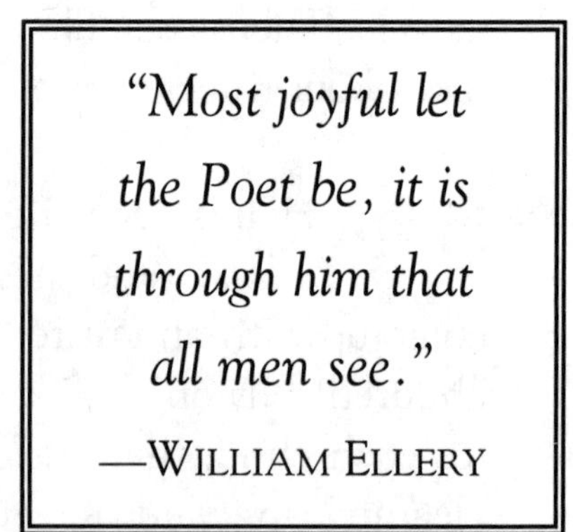

"Most joyful let the Poet be, it is through him that all men see."

—WILLIAM ELLERY

ents this year; you'll pay less than $3 to ship her masterpieces, and I can promise they'll be cherished gifts.

72 An older child (ages seven to ten) might prefer a more "real" looking published book to give to friends or family. Thankfully, there's a new product called Illustory (by Chimeric) that makes it possible for him to produce a professionally edited and typeset hardcover book using his own artwork and text. For about $20, the kit includes a title and dedication page, an "about the author" page, eighteen pages with a box for illustration and lines for text (twelve pages maximum in the published book), an instructional brochure, and a postage-paid envelope for mailing the final manuscript. Your child writes the story, draws accompanying pictures, fills in his author information, designs the cover, then sends his work to the company where it's edited, typeset, and bound into a professional-looking book. Additional copies of the book can be purchased for $18.95. Illustory is available in art and toy stores nationwide.

73 Let's not forget the annual "news" letter for out-of-state family and friends; many families keep in touch sporadically, then write long letters at the end of the year to catch everyone up. Most of the time, these holiday letters are tedious to write (and read), but they're traditional—so why not make it more fun this year? Involve your children. Ask each child to write a special poem, story, or brief essay to include in your newsletter. Buy a roll of black-and-white film and let your third- or fourth-grader snap pictures of everyone during an ordinary day at home. Include photos of family pets. Tape two sheets of typing paper together along the eleven-inch edge using invisible tape and assemble your newsletter by attaching the text and photographs in a pleasing format on both sides. You can run two-sided copies of this "galley" at any reputable print shop for about $.15 each using their paper, or as little as $7 each using your own 11-by-17-inch paper. Ask your children to fold the copies in half, then in thirds, and stuff them into ordinary #10 envelopes for mailing.

74 For quick, inexpensive gifts, ask your children to decorate plain white paper and envelopes with rubber stamps and ink, stickers, or colorful artwork. Let them copy the name and address of the recipient at the top center of each piece of paper, and again in the upper left corner of the envelopes. Slide this stationery into a plain folder, include a package of postage stamps, and voilà: personalized stationery! You can also ship this gift for $3 or less to family or friends who live far away—encouraging them to keep in touch with your children.

75 If your family really excels at one type of project or another, you might want to start a cottage business that everyone can participate in. For example, the greeting cards your little artists design could have computer-printed or calligraphy verses inside, and could be sold through local specialty shops or crafter's malls for up to $2.50 each! Or maybe your holiday newsletter will give birth to a customized newsletter service for area businesses, schools, or organizations. Your young novelist may have so much fun writing and illustrating her own books that you'll find ways to publish more copies of them.

To help you get started making money from your publishing projects, see the Publishing and Business section of the Resource chapter at the end of this book. Be sure to involve your children in the research phase.

CHAPTER

From Boring to Board Games

Arithmetic, computation, or mathematics—no matter what it's called in school, the subject often adds up in a child's mind as plain old *boring*. Kindergarten worksheets display clusters of objects for children to color and count. By third or fourth grade, word problems sneak into the curriculum. I don't know about you, but I remember reading the word problems as a child and thinking, "Who cares?" I also remember spending many happy hours playing board games—several of which teach math skills.

Learning Math Skills in a Roll of the Dice

It's not that the subject of mathematics is boring in and of itself; it's that worksheets, word problems, multiplication tables, and textbooks ignite little (if any) excitement. When your child whines, "This is too *hard,*" what he may really mean is, "This is no *fun!*" Math really can be fun—if you take a less conventional approach to it.

Resist the temptation to buy those supplemental workbooks. By definition, they're work. A better way to learn about math involves rolling dice. Why not pull out one of these games?

76 Boggle Jr. Numbers (Parker Brothers/Milton Bradley) can be fun for the whole family, and it's a great game for an early-elementary-age child. Don't be afraid to involve younger children too. Preschoolers learn to count with the colorful game pieces.

77 Speaking of younger children, generations of toddlers have enjoyed Chutes & Ladders (Milton Bradley). When your little one spins the dial and moves her playing piece, she can count each "step." And, of course, she'll love to "slide" down the chute!

78 Candyland (Milton Bradley) is another all-time favorite board game; maybe you enjoyed it as a child. Did you realize that it taught you basic math skills as you counted your way across the board? It can do the same for your preschooler.

79 Dominoes (Cardinal Industries, Inc.) have dots on them, right? And you have to match up sides that have the same number of dots on each side? You guessed it! Dominoes teach counting, number values, and basic addition and subtraction.

80 Do you remember Yahtzee (Milton Bradley)? That's another fun "math" game! Today Yahtzee is available in a junior version for younger children, too.

81 Mastermind (Pressman Toy Corporation) is a challenging board game that's sure to bring your family hours of fun and learning. Young children might find it difficult, but by pairing a child up with an older player, even little ones can join in.

82 Quarto (Gigamic S.A.) is a math game that's highly recommended by homeschooling families. Using wooden game pieces similar to Dominoes, this game teaches various attributes (such as tall or short, dark or light, round or square, etc.). It isn't always easy to find, and it's a bit expensive at $35 retail, but children love it. The game is available at a reduced retail price (about $28) through Rainbow Resources: 1-888-841-3456.

83 If your kids like Scrabble, they'll love 'Smath. Using equations rather than words, this game teaches addition, subtraction, and division. Game pieces include parentheses, allowing for more complex arrangements of equations. 'Smath can be found at teachers' resource stores and through educational catalogs, such as Chinaberry (1-800-776-2242) or Hearthsong (1-800-325-2502).

84 Hive Alive was developed by an elementary school teacher to provide an energetic way for children to learn math strategy. It's fast-paced, fun, and inexpensive (about $12 retail). The game uses an illustrated honeycomb board, and players move along the hive quickly, learning fractions, decimals, inequalities, negative numbers, and place values. For

For more information about Parker Brothers or Milton Bradley games, contact Hasbro, Inc., Pawtucket, RI 02862. They also carry travel-sized games for portable fun.

more information, write to Aristoplay, Ltd., P.O. Box 7645, Ann Arbor, MI 48107.

Banking on Budgeting Skills with Monopoly

I admit that I still love Monopoly (Parker Brothers). I especially enjoy acting as banker because it's the only time I get to play with that much money! When I was a child, I never thought of Monopoly as "educational"—did you? It was simply great fun. Yet I heard a financial tycoon tell an interviewer that he learned everything he needed to know about money from hours of playing Monopoly as a child. Who knows? Maybe one day your board-game enthusiast will become a leader on Wall Street!

The best thing about board games is that they're anything but boring. Laughing and playing certainly don't seem like "learning," yet games can teach your children many valuable skills. Monopoly lays the foundation for budgeting skills as your children snap up properties, accumulate rent for hotels, or just pass "Go" and collect $200. In addition, your children are fine-tuning their intellectual abilities as they play.

85 Dust off your Monopoly game, push up your sleeves, demand to be the banker, and play a round with your family. Okay, you might have to let someone else be the banker, but encourage everyone to join in. If your children are small, try Monopoly Jr. (Parker Brothers). Or if you're really into *Star Wars*, Monopoly has a *Star Wars* version (Parker Brothers). In fact, there's even an interactive Monopoly game for use with a Sony PlayStation.

86 For more fun with money, try Payday (Parker Brothers/ Milton Bradley). The package says it's geared for children

ages eight and up, but any child who can count will be able to enjoy it. An added benefit is that Payday helps your children get a sense of adult responsibilities—such as bill paying. Perhaps after playing Payday they won't hit you up for a big increase in their allowance!

87 The Game of Life (Parker Brothers/Milton Bradley) teaches similar principles, although this board game is better with third or fourth graders and older. It's not entirely centered around play money, but budgeting skills are integrated into common "life events" as you make your way around the board.

Board games aren't the only ways for children to enjoy learning about money. In fact, toddlers can be introduced to currency values through play. Pretending is a marvelous way to practice skills, and even older children have fun with some of these family activities:

88 Set up a grocery department in one corner of your home. Shelves can be simple and small. Arrange empty food boxes on the shelves, mark prices on them, and open the store for your toddler's enjoyment. You'll need an inexpensive package of play money and a play purse or wallet. Take turns acting as customer and clerk. When your child hands you his selection and money, count out his change the way a cashier would do. Encourage him to do the same when you finish shopping. Of course, he isn't going to be able to count change accurately, but pretending helps him understand the concepts.

89 Start a family bank by purchasing one metal money box for each child. Be sure the boxes lock and that no one other than you has access to the keys. Using a small travel-type

journal, establish a savings "passbook" for each child. When your daughter decides to deposit part (or all) of her allowance, she comes to you—the banker—and her deposit is noted in her passbook. Interest should be accrued monthly, at a rate that's simple to compute (5 percent or 10 percent, depending on your own budget). In order to make a withdrawal, she'll also have to come to the family banker, and the withdrawal is also noted in her passbook. For less than fifteen minutes each month, you can teach any child the basics of savings and interest-bearing accounts.

90 Help your child learn to budget his allowance by providing him with three small plastic storage boxes (such as pencil boxes or baby-wipe boxes) in different colors: one box is designated as "bill money" for things such as bus rides, school lunches, loan payments, and so on; a second box is used for "planned purchases" such as that $90 pair of athletic shoes, video games, and the like; the final box is for "disposable income" or "spending money." You can also get small spiral notepads that fit into the boxes and encourage your child to record deposits and withdrawals from each. Since the boxes are small, they can be stacked easily on a closet shelf or under a bed. Preteens might prefer to use the same type of locked boxes you use for your family bank.

> *"I don't like money, actually, but it quiets my nerves."*
>
> —Joe Louis

91 Try the Ebenezer Scrooge version of Coin Toss: Use a large clean jar or tin can and have each family member toss excess coins into it regularly. One way to encourage this is to earmark all gathered funds for a specific purpose, such as a family vacation, a large purchase, or a favorite charity. At the end of each day or week, coins are tossed into this makeshift bank and it slowly begins to fill. You set a date to harvest, or you can wait until the vessel is overflowing; either way, gather everyone around the kitchen table to sort and roll the coins. Did you know that a family of four can easily collect $50 to $100 in change over a six-month period (even if they haven't been tossing coins in weekly)? Be sure to use your collected funds as you'd been planning.

92 Need a creative way to come up with allowance money when you find yourself running in the red? Use coupons at the grocery store. I know that sounds simplistic, but it isn't. Enlist the help of your children in gathering and clipping coupons for products you normally buy. Ask your children to place their coupons in envelopes with their respective names on them. Pass out the weekly grocery sales section of your newspaper and see if your children can find stores that offer "double coupon" specials. Inform them that you have a certain amount of money to spend. Encourage them to concentrate on coupons that apply to featured sale items. At the grocery store, each child is responsible for locating the grocery items listed on their coupons and totaling up the shelf prices (bring a calculator to help them, or they can use paper and pencils). Once at the checkout, ask the children to give their coupons to the cashier. Write your check for the total amount before the coupons are subtracted, and the change you receive can be distributed to your children accordingly when you return home. For example, if your daughter collected $5 worth of coupons and they were doubled by the store, she'd receive $10 for her allowance. She also gains personal skills in money management and basic math strategy.

Card Sharks and Other Mathematicians

As you can see, you already have plenty of examples to give the next time your child whines, "What do I need to know this for anyway? I'll never use math!" Chances are good the children never realized how much math knowledge they've been acquiring through fun activities and games. Even Wild West poker players were mathematicians of a sort. No, they didn't develop complex equations, but they knew the value of every card and they could count poker chips and money faster than the bartender could fire his gun.

The next time your child complains that math is too hard, dress up Old West style, throw a green tablecloth or towel on your kitchen table, snap a garter on your arm, and deal one of these card games:

Young Children (Ages Three to Six)

93 Go Fish (Mattel)

94 Old Maid (Mattel)

Intermediate Deck Shufflers (Ages Five to Eight)

Rook (Parker Brothers)

Uno (Parker Brothers)

97 Skip Bo (Parker Brothers)

Advanced Card Sharks (Ages Seven to Seventy)

Poker

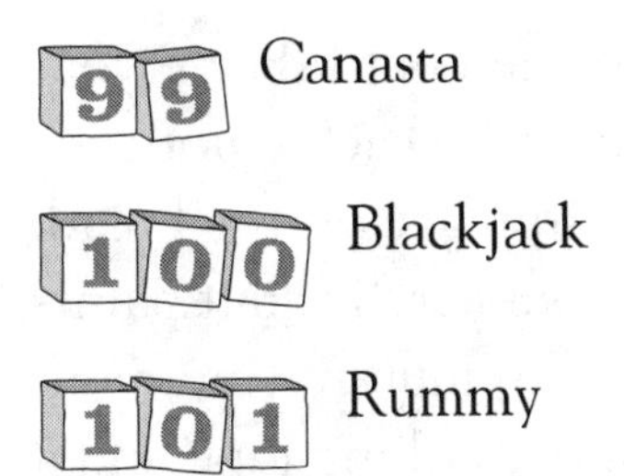

99 Canasta

100 Blackjack

101 Rummy

Of course, card players aren't the only mathematicians of the Wild West—what about those resilient women? The ones who left behind family and convenience for hard work and limited resources? Have you ever looked closely at a patchwork quilt? A mathematician lovingly pieced and stitched that work of art. She probably also designed the pattern, sewed most of the clothes for her family, and created homemade crafts for gift-giving. With all that in mind, here are a few more ideas for your reluctant math student:

102 Start your preschooler off with an easy paint-by-number kit. When your child does paint-by-number, he learns number recognition, spatial properties, and color identification. Many toy and discount stores sell these kits. You can also design your own paint-by-number projects. Begin with a line illustration from a book (or try clip art) and enlarge the image to 8" × 10" at your local copy shop. With a #2 pencil, trace over each black line. Cut a sheet of poster board down to size, or purchase an eight-by-ten-inch canvas board from a craft shop. Place your enlarged and traced copy face down on top of the poster board and

If you haven't played cards for many years, you may want to brush up on the rules or learn a new game. There are a variety of books about card games available through libraries, bookstores, and hobby shops.

use the pencil again to "rub" the lines onto the board. Have your child color the paper copy, then assign a number to each color chosen and write the numbers (with the pencil) in place on the board. Give your child an inexpensive paintbrush. Pour acrylic craft paints (that match the crayon colors) into an old muffin tin; mark each color's number on the tin with a piece of masking tape and a pen. Voilà! Your own paint-by-number kit, personalized for your child.

103 Look for a book about quilting (or quilt designs) in the adult nonfiction section of your public library. Have your child pick a favorite pattern, then help her draw the quilt block on a square piece of poster board. Assign numbers to each color shown in the photograph of the quilt block, and have your child number her drawing. Give her watercolors, markers, or acrylic craft paints, and let her paint her quilt block. When the painting is dry, cut out each patchwork piece to make a personalized homemade puzzle. See how many ways she can arrange the patchwork pieces to create different block designs.

The Dick Blick Art Materials catalog offers a wide range of affordably priced art and craft supplies for children. You can purchase everything from washable markers and paints to felt, beads, specialty papers, glue, scissors—even weaving looms—at an average discount of 10 to 25 percent below list price. This is a reliable company that stands behind its products. To get on the mailing list, write to Dick Blick Art Materials, 695 U.S. Highway 150 East, Galesburg, IL 61401, or call 1-800-447-8192.

104 Design a sampler quilt without ever sewing a stitch. No, this family quilt will not be painted; instead it will be made from craft felt. The foundation piece, cut from felt or any fabric, will need to be large enough to accommodate a quilt block from each member of your family. Ask your children to help you measure and cut the foundation piece, keeping in mind that you'll also want an inch or two of the fabric to show along the edges and between the blocks. Don't worry about exact symmetry; you want this to be more fun than work. Next, have each person pick a favorite patchwork pattern, draw it out on a square piece of paper (approximately 10" × 10" or 12" × 12"), and cut it out. Using various pieces (or scraps) of craft felt, each person uses the pattern pieces as templates, tracing around the template and cutting the piece out of felt. The patchwork pieces are then reassembled and glued to the foundation fabric. When the glue has dried, a two-inch strip of fabric or felt can be stitched along the top of the foundation fabric (from the back side), and a dowel can be inserted for hanging.

105 Make beaded jewelry by purchasing packages of inexpensive (but large) plastic or wooden beads. Have your child calculate how many beads will be needed to make a necklace about twenty inches long and a bracelet about seven inches long. To thread the beads, get some vinyl string (or baby yarn) and a plastic needle, cut the string to size, and let the assembly begin. Have your child double-check her efforts by counting the beads as she strings them, making sure her necklace contains the precalculated number. Finally, tie the ends of the necklace securely.

106 If you're feeling particularly adventurous and generous, have your children help you design and build a playhouse. Every home-improvement store sells books on home projects, and you can draw ideas from one or more of them when designing your own. If the thought of drafting your own plans is intimidating, look for *Playhouses You Can Build.* This book lists projects that range from simple to complex, and full instructions are listed for each project.

107 Arts and crafts aren't the only creative activities that bolster math skills; music lessons teach young children sorting, categorizing, and memory skills. A love of music can ultimately lead to better math grades. If your child shows an interest in music lessons, sign him up for a beginner course. Otherwise, make music together on instruments you create from household materials. You can make simple percussion instruments using clean empty cans, balloons (cut off the narrow end and secure the larger piece to a can using a rubber band), and large rubber bands. Paper plates glued together with dry beans in the center make great "shaker" tambourines. If that's a little too noisy for your jangled nerves at the end of the day, just play instrumental music as you go about your evening routines.

Fun with Food and Fractions

Dinnertime can be difficult in a busy household. At the end of the day you're all tired, cranky, and hungry, but there's still a meal to prepare. When you occasionally involve your children in the preparation of the meal, they learn math. Sounds ridiculous, right? But it's true. Even the simplest recipes call for some form of measurement, and now we're talking fractions! Your child can see that ½ cup is half the size of a full cup, and ¼ cup is half the size of the ½ cup. Get it? Start a few math lessons at the kitchen counter, and you're also getting help with dinner! Besides, if the children are helping you they'll be less inclined to keep whining, "When is dinner gonna be ready?"

Here are a few quick ideas for mealtime math:

108 Line up plastic measuring cups and allow your children to experiment with dry ingredients, such as flour or bread crumbs. Ask them to fill the ¼-cup measure, look at it carefully, then pour it into the ½-cup measure. Talk about what they notice. Next, have them add more of the dry ingredients to the ½-cup measure (until it's full), and then pour it into the 1-cup measure. Again, have them tell you what they observe. Ask a few questions until they make the connection about the relationship between the ¼-cup measure and the 1-cup measure. This is a wonderful exercise to do when your child is having trouble with fractions at school.

109 Make up a batch of biscuit dough and have your children help you roll it out into a large circle. Cut it down the center lengthwise with a knife. Count the pieces with them and ask what they notice (there are now two halves of a circle). Make another cut through the center horizontally. See if they understand that there are now four quarters. Continue cutting, and show them eight eighths and sixteen sixteenths. Roll up the wedges crescent style, and bake them just as you would standard biscuits—but you can call these "fraction rolls." Try the same activity with an apple or orange, and the lesson becomes a yummy snack!

If you cook semiregularly, you'll no doubt come up with other lessons in fractions. The key to success is a willingness to play with your food. Yes, the children might make a bit of a mess, but when they get better math scores you'll be happy they did.

Maybe you're not an aspiring chef and you'd rather not worry about fractions at dinnertime. What about fractions at play? Here are some other ideas to try that don't involve food or dish rags:

110 Legos (Duplo) provide an ideal way to explain fractions and ratios to your children. The same principles that we used with the measuring cups apply. Compare the larger pieces with each of the smaller pieces. Attach smaller top pieces to larger bottom pieces and discuss size relationships in terms of fractions. For example, maybe the red piece is 3" long, the green piece is 1 ½" long, and the white piece is ¾" long—or whole, ½, and ¼ sizes. Because children love Legos, you might find them making faster connections than they did with measuring cups.

> *"I admit that 'twice two makes four' is an excellent thing, but if we are to give everything its due, 'twice two makes five' is sometimes a very charming thing too."*
>
> —Fyodor Dostoyevsky

111 Cut up strips of felt or fabric so that each subsequent piece is half the size of the initial piece, and use the pieces as examples of comparative size relationships.

112 Before a bedtime story, explain to your child that there are a certain number of pages in the book and that you will read half the book one night and half the next. Let him help you figure out how many pages make up half the book. For larger books, you can divide reading sessions into smaller proportions (1/4, 1/6, 1/8, 1/10); have your child not only help you figure out how many pages to read in one session but also how many days it will take you to finish the book.

Math really can be fun and exciting when it's applied to games, creative activities, and everyday experiences.

CHAPTER

From Earth to Sky—Everyday Science

No matter where we lived, my mother always tended to flower beds. If we lived in a cold climate, she'd be out preening, digging, and preparing as soon as the ground thawed. When we had nothing but a twelve-foot-square patio, she bought pots, pebbles, and potting soil at the first hint of spring. Everyone was expected to help with maintenance once the annuals were comfortably tucked in; I admit that pulling weeds was not my favorite Saturday afternoon activity. Mother never called gardening "educational," and I doubt that she ever thought of it that way. For Mom, gardening was about the beauty of blooming colors, and for Pop it meant prizewinning

Beefsteak tomatoes; both of my parents loved to putter with plants.

How Does a Garden Grow?

The toddler who helps her Mommy dig in a flower bed is simply having fun and getting dirty, right? Well, she may be having fun throwing dirt around, but she's also getting an introduction to life sciences. In just a few years, she'll learn:

- How plants grow
- How to distinguish weeds from planned garden inhabitants
- The usefulness of various insects in her backyard ecosystem
- Enough about botany and ecology to design, plan, and grow her own secret (or not-so-secret) garden

Even if she whines about weeding the beds on Saturday afternoons, your child will have gained a wealth of education by simply digging at your side. Who knows? The garden she's tending today could lead to a lucrative career in naturopathic medicine or agricultural development!

Gardening is great for children and adults; it's a lifelong interest you can share. As an activity, gardening provides creativity, structure, physical exercise, personal satisfaction, and tranquillity. As a science, gardening helps us understand and connect with the world we live in. Maybe you already putter among the plants in your landscaped yard, or perhaps you just dream of someday having a large backyard to enjoy. Either way, you and your children can have fun among the flowers. Most of the following ideas don't require a large plot of land to nurture; having been an apartment dweller many times myself, I understand the limitations that small balconies present. You will, however, need at least a child or two, the capacity for play, and a willingness to sometimes get dirty.

113 Plop down in the grass with your child on a sunny day, inhale deeply, and feel the cool blades of grass beneath your fingers. Lie on your stomach and study the palette of colors in a simple patch of green. Count the shades and hues. How many yellows are there? Browns? Greens? Observe tiny insects as they scurry past. How many different kinds do you see? Discuss the subtle differences in the leaf structure of different grasses. Wiggle your fingers down into a thick patch and touch the moist soil. Roll over onto your back and study the sky. Are the clouds fluffy or do they resemble pale ribbons across the sky? Is the sky really blue? Are clouds really white? If the sky is cloudless, what does its color remind you of? Do you remember why you enjoyed experiencing all of this when you were a child? Share those memories with your child.

114 Go for a walk around your neighborhood during the late spring or early summer months. How many different kinds of flowers, shrubs, and trees can you and your children identify? Take along a pocket book of gardening from a local bookstore to help you name as many as possible. What are the most popular flowers in your area? Do they look fresh and healthy? Make a mental note of what is or isn't growing well.

115 Press your family's favorite flowers in sheets of tissue the old fashioned way—wedged between the pages of a thick book. When pressed and dry, use them in nature crafts such as decoupage greeting cards, homemade paper stationery, or resin jewelry.

116 To make homemade paper, recycle junk mail and/or paper grocery bags by cutting the paper into strips and soaking it for half an hour or so in a large bowl of warm water. Pour the pulpy paper and water into your kitchen blender and pulse until smooth. Pour this solution onto a wire frame or a stack of paper towels, drop a pressed flower or two onto the wet pulp, and squeeze out the excess water by firmly pressing a dry sponge on top of the pulp. The flowers become part of the paper!

117 Start a family journal of seasons in a simple spiral notebook. When does the growing season officially start in your area? March 21 is Spring Equinox (when the sun reaches its halfway point along its yearly journey north), but you may still have snow on the ground in your area. The first day you notice that grassy areas are greening, make a note in your journal. When do the daffodils bloom? Note that, too. Summer should bring a flurry of birds to any area in North America; jot down the ones you see each day. Record weather patterns and temperatures throughout the seasons. As summer fades, notice when local trees begin to turn color. When is the peak of fall color? When are deciduous trees finally bare? Jot down the date of the first snowfall or winter rains. How long does your winter last?

Papermaking is both fun and educational. You can purchase basic kits, individual wire frames or molds, packaged pulp, and instructional books through arts and crafts stores. Some toy store chains also sell paper-making kits for children. Zainy Brainy offers a product called Paper Anew; these kits run between $20 and $25 and come with complete instructions.

118 Speaking of winter, when drizzly days or arctic winds bring cabin fever to your household, pour some hot chocolate and browse through a stack of seed catalogs. W. Atlee Burpee & Co. has been around for many years and their annual publications are bright enough to lift the grayest spirits on a cold, yucky day. Write to them at P.O. Box 5114, Warminster, PA 18974-4818 for a free catalog. Harris Seeds is another reputable company, and you can write to them at 60 Saginaw Drive, P.O. Box 22960, Rochester, NY 14692-2960. If you love old-fashioned flowers, send your name, address, and $1 (U.S.) for the catalog to Select Seeds, 180 Stickney Hill Road, Union, CT 06076.

119 For a splash of fresh flowers at holiday time, help your children force bulbs during the autumn months. This is easy to do; instead of sinking bulbs into fall flower beds, place them in a paper sack and slide them into the back of your refrigerator for two to four weeks. After their "winter rest" in the refrigerator, nestle them into small clay pots filled with potting soil, water them, and place them in a dark, cool closet for a few more days before setting them on a sunny windowsill or table. Within a month, you'll have an abundance of colorful blooms, and your children will have watched the growth process in a way that's not always possible outdoors. To order inexpensive bulbs,

Garden Magic Kids, part of The National Children's Garden Registry, offers contests, programs, newsletters, products, and free seeds for children of all ages. Your aspiring Victory Gardener will love the activities, which were designed to encourage an interest in natural sciences. For more information, call 1-800-431-SOIL.

write for a free catalog from Michigan Bulb Co., 1950 Waldorf NW, Grand Rapids, MI 49550.

120 Begin your family garden early by sowing seeds in egg cartons at the end of winter. Spoon a bit of potting soil into each section of the egg carton and plant the seeds according to package instructions. Keep the germinating seeds moist until the first sprouts appear, then place them in a sunny area, watering them every two or three days as needed. By the time the ground outside is workable, you'll be well on your way to a spectacular show of vegetables and flowers.

"Flowers have an expression of countenance as much as men or animals. Some seem to smile, some have a sad expression, some are pensive and diffident, others are plain, honest, and upright."

—HENRY WARD BEECHER

121 Preteen children like to explore subjects deeply, and that includes gardening. They want to know more than "how-to"; they want to learn all those things that their parents don't know. For example, why are certain flowers named they way they are? Where did the names come from? What ancient lore is attached to various flowers? An entertaining book that can help answer those questions is *100 Flowers and How They Got Their Names*. Going beyond the origins of familiar plant names, the book ventures into history, society, ancient lore, and comical facts that few gardening enthusiasts are ever aware of. Your adolescent will delight in his ability to "one-up" you with facts about flowers.

122 Plant a potted herb garden on your patio or balcony. Several specialty stores sell herb kits, but you can save money by purchasing a half-dozen pots, pebbles (for drainage), potting soil, and a few packets of seeds. Use your fresh herbs for cooking, or harvest them and then hang them upside down in a warm, dry place for a few days. Crush the dried leaves and store them in airtight containers. Dried herbs can be used to flavor salt or vinegar—both of which make great gifts for friends and family.

123 Create potpourri sachets and hot pads from your dried herbs by securing a small handful of the herbs in layers of cheesecloth or other light cotton cloth. For sachets, place the herbs in the center of a square of fabric, pull the corners to the center, hold the herbs in place, twist the cloth, and tie it with string. Hot pads protect countertops while providing a delightful aroma, and they're easy to make: Cut two equal rectangles of cotton fabric and stitch them together along three sides; pour in a generous amount of dried herbs, turn under the unstitched

Make flavored salt or vinegar simply and easily by adding a few sprigs of dried herbs (such as basil, rosemary, or thyme) to clean, pretty jars containing ordinary table salt or white vinegar. You can flavor light oils in the same manner. *Low-Fat, High-Flavor Cookbook* (Oxmoor House, 1995) contains several delicious recipes for gourmet oils, rubs, spice blends, and vinegars. This book is available for about $20 through Southern Progress Corporation, P.O. Box 2463, Birmingham, AL 35201. You can also browse through *Cooking Light* and *Food & Wine* magazines for simple, savory recipes.

side, and secure with blanket stitching; "quilt" the hot pad at one- or two-inch intervals with small stitches, and it's ready for use.

124 Help your children make herbal soaps. Have them measure 2 cups of water, 2 cups of soap flakes (from old soaps or purchased at a craft shop), and 1 to 2 ounces of glycerin (available in most drug stores) into a small pot. Bring the mixture to a boil over medium heat, stirring constantly (an adult should do this part!). Sprinkle a few teaspoons of dried or fresh herbs into the liquid soap, and continue to boil gently until the scent of the herbs fills the kitchen. Remove the pot from the stove, pour the liquid into muffin tins or molds, and chill them in the refrigerator for a few hours. Unmold the soaps and wrap them in colorful tissue paper or plastic wrap.

125 You can also make scented candles from herbs by melting paraffin wax (or wax chips) in a glass container in your microwave oven; stir in the herbs and heat for another minute at medium power. To make these candles on your stovetop, melt the wax over low heat in an old, medium-sized pot, stirring constantly. Add your herbs. Next, place candle wicks (available from your local arts and crafts stores) in the center of muffin tins and add the melted wax. Place the muffin tin in the freezer for fifteen minutes or more so that the candles will pop out easily. Again, children should be kept away from the hot wax—but they will certainly enjoy assisting in the preparations!

126 For natural watercolor paints, pluck the vibrant petals from several garden flowers, crush them slightly, place them in microwave-safe tea cups, cover them with water (about ¼" deep), place the cups in the microwave, and cook them at the highest setting for two to three minutes. Leave the cups in the microwave for several minutes to cool. When you remove them, use a small spoon to gather and discard the flower petals. The water in the cups will retain the color of the petals. This helps even very young children understand where colors come from, and they can have fun painting with the homemade brew; just be sure they don't drink it!

127 Plants aren't the only things found in gardens. Children are often fascinated with bugs, and you can help them observe local insect communities without bringing the critters into your home. Most toy stores and nature shops sell very inexpensive "bug boxes"—plastic contraptions that have a magnified end for viewing a captured insect. When your child finds an interesting bug, she places it in the observation box and is able to get a closer look without harming the creature. Of course, the way you and I did it years ago still works today: help your child make a "bug box" by adding small air holes to the lid of a clean jar. Be sure to add a few leaves and twigs to the jar if your child plans to extend her observations for a day or two. Also, if the jar is kept outside, have her place it out of direct sunlight (which will fry the bug in short order).

128 Experience the mystery of butterflies together. On a cool spring morning, gather a few clean, large jars (with tiny holes punched into the lids) and a bucket. Head for a wooded area. Instruct your children to be on the lookout for caterpillars; you'll notice them on the back sides of leaves, on tree trunks, or at the edges of wild flowers. Carefully lift a few and place them in jars. Gather some soil from the area and scoop it into the bucket; add a few twigs, leaves, and other types of plant life. At home, transfer the soil and foliage to a small- to medium-sized

terrarium (or empty aquarium). Gently place the caterpillars in their new environment, then cover the terrarium with a large panel of cheesecloth (secured to the side of the terrarium with tape or rubber bands). The caterpillars will eat the vegetation; any that don't eat in the first few days should be brought back outside. Within a few days or weeks, the caterpillars will begin to spin cocoons. Once cocooned, the transformation will begin. Just before the caterpillar emerges as a butterfly, the cocoon will begin to wiggle. Soak a gauze pad with sugar water and place it in the terrarium. As the butterfly emerges, she dries her wings. Then she'll sip the nectar. After a day or two, take the terrarium outside, open it up, and release your butterfly.

129 The Midwest is home to several kinds of cattails. These plants grow in marshy areas and along country highways; they can get up to ten feet high and are wonderful to examine. They're also useful for arts and crafts. Help your child snip a few cattails at summer's end. Fresh cattails can be used as paintbrushes for interesting effects. You can preserve cattails by spraying them with polyurethane or dipping them in a bucket that has a mixture of water and acrylic gloss medium (one part medium to two parts water). Allow them to dry completely by attaching the stem to a metal shirt hanger with a clothespin, placing the hanger out of the way. Preserved cattails can be used in flower arrangements or collages.

130 Autumn foliage is spectacular, and we sometimes wish the beauty would last more than a few short weeks. Your children can keep the memory of a special autumn day by creating a fallen-leaf collage. It all begins with a walk in the park;

bring along a paper bag. Help your child gather as many kinds of leaves you can find. For example:

- Wild cherry leaves are glossy, elongated, and russet-colored, with saw-toothed edges
- Dogwood leaves are oval, deep-veined, and brighter red

- Oak leaves have five to nine lobes and are more brown in color
- Maple leaves have wide, pointed lobes that are red, yellow, or orange
- Elm leaves are similar in shape to dogwood (oval), but have saw-toothed edges and are yellow-brown
- Birch leaves look a lot like elm, but are bright yellow in color

- Cottonwood leaves are triangular, usually blemished, and golden

- Ginkgo leaves are fan-shaped, delicate-looking, and green-gold

Your area might have other species, but you get the idea. When you've gathered and discussed the leaves, cover your kitchen table with newspaper or a vinyl cloth and lay out a sheet of bright blue poster board. Dip each leaf in a mixture of equal parts water and wood glue—white glue also works, but wood glue works best. Place each dipped leaf on the poster board, making an interesting design. The glue not only acts as an adhesive but helps to preserve the leaves for several weeks or months.

131 Plant a tree that your child has grown from seed. Together, collect seeds from apples, cherries, pears, peaches, or other fruits, and don't forget about maple seeds or acorns that you find on the ground. Have your child mark several small containers—each with the name of a different seed—and fill them with slightly rocky soil from your yard. Next, ask your child to poke his finger into the center of each container and bury two to three seeds in each hole. Place the containers in a sunny location and water the soil lightly every three or four days. At least one container should produce a seedling; when the seedling is almost eight inches high, transplant it to a larger pot. Fertilize the tiny tree no more than once every two months. Within a year (or at about eighteen inches in height), the tree should be ready to plant in a sheltered area of your yard. Support it with a stick or pole if necessary and watch it grow as your child grows.

132 Urban dwellers can beautify local neighborhoods by forming a grassroots renewal effort, such as a community garden or a park beautification project. Involve as many families as possible and enlist the help of public schools. Begin by choosing a specific project and contacting local authorities. If your area doesn't have an urban renewal agency, you can contact John Lewis at The Bank of Fayetteville, One South Block, Fayetteville, AR 72701, for more information about launching one in your community.

Chemistry Begins in the Kitchen

If life science begins in a flower bed, then physical science begins at the kitchen counter. While you were baking cookies with your mother, you were also learning basic principles of chemistry and physics. If that statement raised an eyebrow, think about the following questions:

- Did you carefully (or semicarefully) measure the flour, sugar, baking powder, baking soda, and salt into a bowl? [chemistry, step one]
-  Did you combine wet ingredients with dry ones to make a consistent batter? [chemistry, step two]
- Did you measure that batter onto a cookie sheet? [physics, step one]
- Once in the oven, did you peek in and watch the dough spread and rise? [physics, step two]

Chances are good that, when you were eight or nine, all you really thought about was how delicious those cookies were going to taste. You weren't thinking about chemistry or physics. I'll bet your mother wasn't either, but you were learning the basics in spite of your fun. Science really can be as fun and easy as baking a batch of chocolate chip cookies. Here are a few experiments for your family to try:

133 Dust off your great-grandmother's cookie recipe, gather the necessary ingredients, call the children into the kitchen, and spend an evening baking. While the dry ingredients are being measured, pull two glasses down from the cabinet and fill them halfway with water; set them on the counter. Ask your child to measure 1 teaspoon of baking powder and pour it into one of the glasses of water. As the water bubbles, explain to her that the same kind of air bubbles form in the dough as it's cooking, causing the cookie to rise. Next, ask her to measure 1 teaspoon of baking soda and drop it into the other glass. Nothing will happen. Now

add a little bit of juice (any kind will work) to the water, and bubbles will appear. Explain that baking soda looks a lot like baking powder and they do similar things, but baking soda reacts to acids (contained in the juice) instead of bases. If your child seems intrigued, you can look up more information in an encyclopedia while the cookies are baking.

1 3 4 Experiment with a Sourdough Starter and recipes. You'll need a clean,one-quart glass or plastic container with a lid. Air circulation is important, so carefully punch a few holes in the lid. Next, dissolve ¾ cup of sugar and 1package of active dry yeast in 1 cup of very warm (not hot) water. Stir in 3 tablespoons of instant potato flakes, cover, and store in the refrigerator for several days.

Delicious and easy sourdough bread will fill your home with aroma. Before bed, combine 4–5 cups of flour, ⅓ cup of sugar, and 1 tablespoon of salt in a large mixing bowl. To this, add ½ cup of canola oil and 1 cup of Sourdough Starter. Mix well. Knead the dough on a lightly floured surface for a few minutes until ingredients are well combined and dough is elastic. Place the dough in a bowl that has been coated with cooking oil spray, cover with plastic wrap, and allow to rise overnight. Punch the dough down in the morning, divide it in half, shape each half into a loaf, place the loaves in two lightly oiled glass loaf pans, and set them on the center rack of your cold oven. About an hour later, turn on the oven (set at 350 degrees), and bake for thirty to thirty-five minutes, until golden brown. Remove the loaves from the pans immediately. Cool on wire racks or paper towels.

Each day, take a peek at the mixture with your children. The starter is ready when the surface is frothy and the mixture smells like potato liqueur. Remove the starter from the refrigerator, allow it to sit for one hour, and "feed" it with another ¾ cup of sugar, 3 tablespoons of potato flakes, and 1 cup of warm water. Once fed, the brew should rest, uncovered, at room temperature for eight to twelve hours. Return it to the refrigerator for a few days until you're ready to bake. Explain the fermentation process to your children, or look it up together in an encyclopedia. Compare the bubbles in the starter with the bubbles produced by baking powder or baking soda.

135 For no-bake, rainy-day fun, try making flour plaster and casting your child's handprint. You'll need 1 cup of flour, ½ cup of table salt, and ½ cup of water. Mix all the ingredients together until you have a dough-like consistency. Help your child roll the dough into a ball shape, then flatten it slightly by pressing the ball between the countertop and a dinner plate. Lightly flour your child's palm and have her press an imprint of her hand into the center of the dough. Using a pencil, poke a hole through the top of the plaque and allow it to dry for several days. Discuss the drying process (evaporation) with your child. A light coating of acrylic sealer will protect the plaque, or your child can paint it first with tempera.

136 Make your own play clay for a fraction of the cost of ready-made versions. Heat 1 ¼ cups of water in a medium pot over medium heat on the stove until just below the boiling point (children should be kept at a safe distance). Stir in 1 cup of cornstarch and 2 cups of baking soda, and cook until the mixture has thickened. Remove the pot from the stove and allow it to cool. When the batch of dough is warm (not hot), have your child work in a few drops of food coloring. Explain that, since cornstarch and baking soda are both "base" ingredients, the baking soda will not cause the dough to rise. Divide out a small portion of the colored dough, place it in a bowl, and have your child work in 1 teaspoon of vinegar. He should notice a slight fizz as he works it in; this is the effect of an acid combining with a base, and depending on the type of food coloring used, the dough might change color as well. When your child has washed his hands, he'll have a good-sized lump of play clay to enjoy. Keep the clay soft between uses by placing it in a plastic bag and storing it in the refrigerator.

137 Your child can make homemade putty by mixing ½ cup of cornstarch with 1 tablespoon of white glue. She should knead the putty well. Once mixed, the putty can be worked into shapes. Have her press it onto a piece of printed newspaper; when she lifts the putty, the newsprint lettering will be visible on the underside because the glue and the cornstarch have worked together (chemically) to absorb some of the ink. Have her hold this up in front of a mirror and examine the print. Homemade putty can also be kept for several weeks in a plastic bag in the refrigerator.

138 Next time you cook cabbage, reserve some of the juice from the pot. When the juice has cooled, have your child paint a design with it on white paper. When the painting is dry, have him paint on top of the design with vinegar or grape juice; the color of the original painting will "magically" transform before his eyes! Explain that cabbage juice is an acid/base indicator, which means that it shows the acidity of a liquid by changing color on white paper when acid is present. Try the experiment again (with a fresh sheet of paper), but brush milk over the dry cabbage-juice painting. Ask him what he has noticed about the vinegar in contrast to the milk.

139 Lemon juice and white grape juice are excellent "invisible" inks. Have your child paint with either of these juices on plain white paper. When the painting is dry, any design will be barely visible. But when the paper is placed in a warm oven (175 to 200 degrees) for a few minutes (by an adult), the design will magically appear in a golden-brown hue. Explain that the sugars in the juice have carbonized when heated, turning brown. You can also allow the "invisible" painting to dry in a sunny window; in a few days, the design will turn light golden-brown from the heat of the sun.

140 Speaking of painting, when the weather is nasty, the children are whining, and you're out of watercolor paints, your children can make their own nontoxic casein paints. Before you assemble the supplies, explain that all paints are made from pigments and binders (binders help the pigments stick to the painting surface). For example, watercolor paints are made from dry pigments, gum arabic, and water; acrylic paints are made from the same pigments with a liquid plastic (acrylic) compound; oil paints are made from pigments mixed with linseed oil. Many years ago, painters mixed their own paints with colored minerals (pigments) and egg yolks or milk curd. Paint made from egg yolks is called "egg tempera," and paint made with milk is called "casein paint." Give each child an ice cube tray and let them pour a little evaporated milk into the wells. Next, add a few drops of food

> *"No amount of experimentation can prove me right; a single experiment can prove me wrong."*
>
> —Albert Einstein

coloring to each well and stir. Experiment with the colors to make purples, oranges, browns, and other colors. Finally, spread out plain white paper and have fun. The paintings will dry to a semigloss finish as a result of the milk fat.

141 Make your own sherbet on a hot summer day by stirring together a 13-ounce can of evaporated milk, an 8-ounce can of frozen lemonade concentrate (thawed), and a few drops of yellow food coloring. Place the bowl in the freezer for one hour, remove, and stir; return the bowl to the freezer until the sherbet is soft-set. For comparison, dissolve 2 or 3 tablespoons of salt in 2 cups of warm water and place that bowl in the freezer as well. When the sherbet is ready to eat, the salt water will still be liquid. Return the salt water to the freezer and leave it for twenty-four hours or more. Check it again. What do your children notice? If you live in an area with cold winters, your children will begin to understand why snowy roads are salted.

142 Children love soap bubbles, and you can save money by having them make their own solution with ½ cup of liquid detergent, 2 quarts of water, and 2 teaspoons of sugar or corn syrup. Aside from blowing bubbles with the mixture, you can try a few other experiments together. First, place some of the liquid in a 13-by-9-inch pan, add a few drops of food coloring, and stir. Have a piece of white paper ready, then have your child create a froth of bubbles in the pan by blowing carefully into the liquid with a straw. Quickly touch the surface of the paper to the bubbles without immersing the paper in the liquid. The shape of the bubbles will be captured on the paper in a colorful abstract design, and you can discuss how touching the surface of a bubble releases the air within it. Create frozen bubbles on a frigid day by blowing bubbles

outdoors the same way you do in warm weather; if the temperature is cold enough, your child will see that the bubbles instantly become balls of ice crystals.

You can get additional ideas for fun and experimentation from library books. A good title to look for is *Beginning Science*. Don't forget cookbooks as a resource for kitchen science!

A Telescope Can Take Your Child Beyond This Earth

Have you ever said the words, "Star light, star bright, first star I see tonight . . ."? Have you ever searched for a shooting star? Have you ever watched the moon rise—or tried to make out the craters on its glowing surface? Do you know the pattern of the Big Dipper, and do you look for it now and then? As a child, were you interested in space exploration? Did you wonder what it would be like to be an astronaut—to travel beyond the limits of our atmosphere?

Science doesn't begin and end with the world we live in; your child can explore the universe for about $50. Any toy store or toy department sells inexpensive telescopes for beginning astronomers, and you'll have hours of stargazing fun together when you buy one. Even tiny children enjoy a clearer view of the twinkling night sky.

When you're looking for a suitable telescope, keep in mind that an expensive model is not always the best choice for family fun; look for a durable model in a moderate price range. There are three types to choose from:

- Refractive telescopes use a lens to collect light and bend it, which brings the viewed object into focus
- Catadioptric telescopes use a corrective lens and two mirrors to achieve a similar effect

- Reflective telescopes use a mirror to collect the light, and then reflect the light to another mirror (via a special concave shape), which brings the object into focus through the eyepiece

Refractive telescopes are the most widely available, and you're likely to find this type in a toy store. Library books can help you and your children decide which kind of telescope fits your needs and budget. Lenses vary in magnification (more powerful telescopes can be pricey), but even a low-end telescope can provide a good viewing field. Expect to pay $35 to $75 for a basic, durable model. It's a small price to pay for years of enjoyment.

The following activities will get you started while you're looking for a family telescope:

143 Chart the phases of the moon during a one-month period. Using a drinking glass as a template, draw seven circles on blue paper and cut them out. Do the same thing with yellow paper. The first night, gaze at the moon together and cut the lighted shape of the moon from a yellow circle to match what you see. Paste a blue circle on another piece of paper, then paste the yellow shape over the blue "moon"; date the page. Continue your nightly ritual, repeating the process with each lunar phase. A new moon is dark (all blue), a new crescent has a narrow yellow slice on the right side, the first-quarter moon is half yellow (also on the right side), a new gibbous moon is three quarters yellow (right side), the full moon is all yellow, and the remaining lunar phases (old gibbous, last quarter, and old crescent) mirror the first phases with the yellow area on the left side. The entire cycle should take twenty-nine to thirty days. If your family observes a second full moon during the same month, you have experienced a true "blue moon."

144 Gather a globe, a flashlight, a small ball, and a lamp to create a lunar eclipse. Shine the lamp directly on the globe, tape a string to the ball, and have your child dangle this "moon" behind the globe. Turn out any other lights in the room. The dark side of the globe represents night. When the ball is directly behind the globe, the "moon" is in complete shadow; your child is getting a close look at a lunar eclipse. Have a little fun with this by trying to duplicate the earth orbiting around the sun and the moon orbiting around the earth.

145 Make a Milky Way mobile together and hang it in your child's room. Begin by painting the bottoms of two paper plates with dark blue or black water-based paint (such as tempera). When the dark paint has dried, add small white and yellow dots in a spiral pattern to one of the plates. Punch a small hole in the center of the other plate. Pull one end of a two- to three-foot section of string through the punched hole and tape the bottom inch to the white side of the plate. Place both plates together evenly (white sides in). Glue, tape, or staple the edges of the plates together. The starry side should face down, and the string side will be on top. Hang the mobile from the ceiling; as it spins gently, it mimics the night sky. For a luminous effect, use fluorescent paints to make the stars; the mobile will glow in the dark.

146 Learn about space and astronomy by playing The Game of SPACE. This card game is fun, entertaining, and inexpensive as well as educational. Developed by a science teacher, it's geared toward children ages eight and up, but younger children can join in when paired with an adult. See the end of this chapter for information about obtaining this and other games from Other Worlds Educational Enterprises.

147 Study the stars on a clear night and see how many constellations you and your child can identify. A library book or two can help you recognize the dot-to-dot patterns. Try this first without a telescope, then with one. The difference is amazing!

Family Science Expeditions in Unexpected Places

Science museums, planetariums, and zoos are obvious choices for educational family fun. For example, residents of the Columbus, Ohio area flock to COSI (a science museum) throughout the year, and Zoologist Jack Hanna, a Columbus native, is a local legend at the Columbus Zoo. Children and parents alike love these places for good reason: they're fun. They're not, however, the only places where science spills into recreation.

148 Next time your family is on a picnic, explore the scientific possibilities. When ants come marching in, study them to watch where they take your crumbs of food. Observe nature and weather while you eat or play. Invite discussion by asking your child leading questions, such as "How many kinds of trees can you see from here?" Collect picnic souvenirs, such as pine cones, rocks, leaves, or feathers. When you're throwing the Frisbee back and forth, talk about gravity and inertia. Ditto with a football. Study leaf litter and discuss erosion, composting, and how both affect the environment. Catch a few bugs and study them in a "bug box" or jar before setting them free (see activity 127 earlier in this chapter). The possibilities are almost endless.

149 Follow in Simon and Garfunkle's footsteps and walk off to look for America: explore our vast wealth of walking trails and national parks during family vacations. Begin with your

local area; if you're visiting out-of-state relatives or friends, introduce your children to the natural habitats there. *The Essential Guide to Nature Walking in the United States* lists more than 2,500 easy, family-friendly trails from the Atlantic to the Pacific. The author includes addresses for further information. He also provides terrain information, hike lengths, and descriptions of wildlife for every park. All fifty states are included, as well as tips on recommended clothing, gear, and food for family hiking safety and enjoyment.

150 If outdoor excursions don't appeal to you, consider a factory tour. Virtually any factory offers lessons in science of one kind or another. If you love chocolate, imagine touring the Hershey plant in Pennsylvania. Your children could learn all about chocolate manufacturing and packaging (chemistry, physics, and engineering)—and what a delicious way to do it! If your children are crayon fans, visiting a crayon factory would be ideal. Does your son or daughter love rock and roll? Visit a guitar company. Is your child a bookworm? Tour a paper factory. Scout out various factories of interest in your vicinity and call to arrange a tour.

151 Artists are certainly creative people, but they're also scientists and engineers. Science is involved in art from the manufacture of paint, to mixing colors on a palette, to pushing and pulling the paints on canvas or paper in expression of the artist's vision. Every pigment, every medium, every surface leads back to science. A day spent visiting an artist's studio is educational on many levels. It's also a fascinating experience for any child who is artistically inclined. Call your local arts council or art league; ask if any members allow studio visits. If you can arrange a visit with a local artist, be sure to discuss with your children all the interesting elements and surprises you discover in the studio.

152 Do you have a favorite family restaurant? Call the owner or manager to see if you can arrange a behind-the-scenes tour for your children. You might want to dabble in some kitchen science before the visit in order to associate lessons learned at the kitchen counter with the career of a restaurant chef.

153 Do you have a photo-processing store nearby? Ask the manager if your children can watch as a roll of film is developed and printed. Encourage your children to ask questions during the process.

154 Are your children animal enthusiasts? Look under the heading "Animal Breeders" in the Yellow Pages of your telephone book and arrange a personal visit for your family. Have your children compose a list of questions to ask the breeder.

155 Is there a small jewelry shop near your home? See if the resident appraiser is willing to explain the process of assessment to your budding gemologist.

156 Visit an auto body shop and watch as a car is painted or windows are tinted. Again, encourage your child to ask questions.

157 If you're raising a young Frank Lloyd Wright, drop in at a print shop that handles architectural blueprints. Ask the owner or manager for a few minutes of time to explain how a blueprint is made.

158 A florist can explain how flowers are kept fresh for days in the shop, how they're placed in arrangements, and how they are later transported to fulfill orders.

159 Have you ever visited a Christmas tree farm? Farmers are scientists, too. Off-season provides an opportunity to explore the farm more thoroughly (with permission, of course). You might even offer your family's services during planting in order to get a first-hand experience of life on the farm.

160 Spend a Saturday afternoon at an aquarium shop and plan a small family aquarium of tropical fish. Page through the books and magazines at the store to brush up on what equipment you'll need. Give your children plenty of time to enjoy every colorful tank; point out the exotic fish and have everyone pick favorites. Don't plan to buy anything during your first excursion. Instead, plan on taking a few weeks or months to prepare for making the right purchases.

161 Next time you have a dental appointment, see if you can schedule a little extra time to learn more about the science of dentistry. Maybe your dentist or dental hygienist will be happy to give your family a brief tour.

162 Contact your local gas or electric company to see if they offer any programs on energy conservation. Occasionally the companies offer brief seminars; ask if they have a version that's used in public schools. Plan on attending an event that's appropriate for your child's age and interest level.

Don't forget excursions that can happen in your own home through videos and games:

- *The Best Of Beakman's World*, Columbia TristarVideo
- *Bill Nye The Science Guy*, Disney Home Video

- *Kratt's Creatures*, Poly Gram Video
- *National Geographic Kids' Really Wild Animals*, Columbia Tristar Video
-  *The Nova Series*, Time-Life Video
- *Poop, Paw, and Hoofprints*, Victorian Video Productions (see company information in Chapter 6)

The Game of EARTH, The Game of SPACE, and The Game of OCEAN, card games by Other Worlds Educational Enterprises, P.O. Box 6193, Woodland Park, CO 80866; individual games sell for $10 each, and all three sell for $29.

CHAPTER

Welcome to the Computer Age

If computers don't appeal to you, or if using one has been frustrating, you might be tempted to skip to the next chapter. That would be okay *if* computers weren't becoming such a necessary tool for business and education. Did you know that a few of the largest national daycare chains now have computers in the classrooms? Or that some two-year-olds are learning to write at the keyboard before they can manipulate a pencil? Just about every grade school in this country offers computer time for all students, and computer literacy is part of today's elementary education. Some public schools even subscribe to online services and teach children how to "surf the Net."

When personal computers hit the market several years ago, skeptics insisted that they'd be impossible to sell. Why would any family want a large piece of electronic machinery cluttering up a desk? Why would anyone be interested in learning a complex "computer language"? Why would a family want to spend that much money? Indeed, the first-generation PCs were oversized, overpriced, and a bit overwhelming. Do you remember the DOS operating system?

What Can You Do with a Home Computer?

Today's personal computers are a far cry from their ancestors, and families all over the world are buying them in record numbers; some homes have more than one. Why? Computers make our lives easier, are now fun to use, and are more affordable than in the past. How do they make our lives easier? Well, with a personal computer, a range of software, and a modem, you can:

- Balance your family budget
- Keep accurate personal records
- Plan everything from menus to remodeling
- Send greetings to friends and relatives
- Chart your family tree
- Track down friends from long ago
- Do your banking and bill-paying electronically
- Design a garden—and see how it will grow before you invest any money in materials
- Plan your next vacation (and book the reservations with the click of a mouse)
- Review your diet and design a custom fitness regime
-  Research medical problems

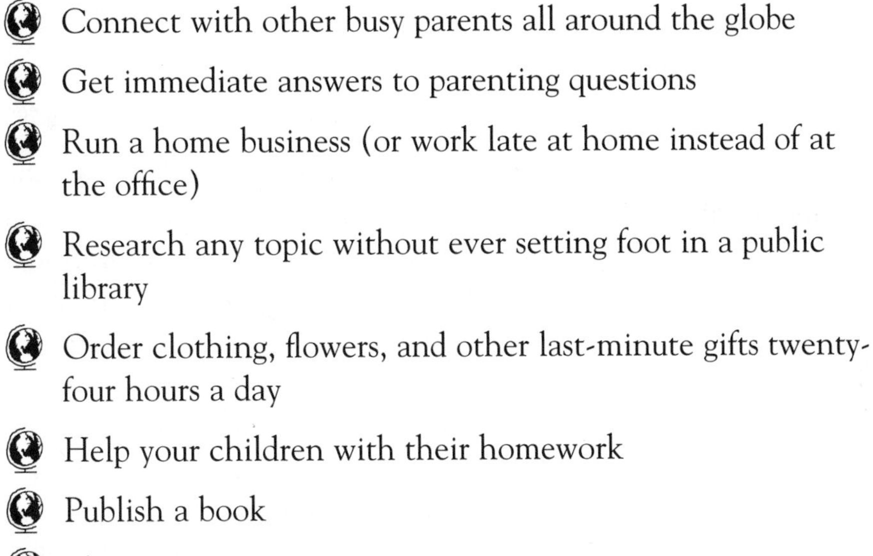

- Review restaurants
- Connect with other busy parents all around the globe
- Get immediate answers to parenting questions
- Run a home business (or work late at home instead of at the office)
- Research any topic without ever setting foot in a public library
- Order clothing, flowers, and other last-minute gifts twenty-four hours a day
- Help your children with their homework
- Publish a book
- Play games
- "Chat" with a friend in another state for a fraction of the price of a long-distance phone call
- Find a job (through Internet job banks)
- Find a partner
- Read your favorite newspapers and magazines
- Review mortgage options and apply for a loan
- "Tour" places you're interested in seeing (an art museum, the Vatican, etc.)
- Program your home so that the lights come on while you're vacationing
- Buy your groceries and have them delivered
- Make customized items (such as T-shirts, calendars, etc.)

- Play a round of golf
- Attend college and earn a degree
- And more!

As technology explodes and software choices expand, it's possible to do more and more with a personal computer. Some models can answer your phone, play music as you work, send a fax, and organize your favorite photographs. Of course a computer like that will cost a bundle . . . until the next wave of more powerful machines is introduced.

What if you don't have a computer? It's easy enough to find one. Department stores nationwide stock PCs; they're convenient, but you won't always get the best price. Computer superstores are another option; their "package" systems are generally advertised between $1,000 and $3,000. However, if you're willing to spend a little time doing research, you can set up a reasonably functional system for as little as $600. Here's how:

- Look for a gently used 286 or 386 computer at garage sales, pawn shops, or computer resellers; expect to pay between $100 and $200 for the system and monitor
- Research prices at local Mom-and-Pop computer stores that offer upgrade packages; expect to pay anywhere from $200 to $350 to upgrade a 286 into a system with Pentium power and a CD-ROM
- Invest in a high-quality surge-protection strip; these run from $15 to $30
- Purchase a fax-modem of no less speed than 14,400 bps; low-end modems run about $50

- Subscribe to an Internet Service Provider (ISP), such as America Online or CompuServe (both provide Internet access, searchable databases, chat functions, forum support, etc.)
- Purchase a good ink-jet or laser printer, new or used. A basic, new ink-jet printer runs about $200 (used ones cost anywhere from $75 to $100), while a basic laser printer will cost about $300 (used ones cost from $100 to $150)
- Buy only the software you can reasonably expect to use; don't overlook previous versions, which are generally upgradable and more cost-effective than the latest versions

Another way to buy a computer (or get one free) is to check with small companies that are going out of business or large corporations that are upgrading the computer systems in their offices. Finding such an opportunity is not as uncommon as it might sound; many midsize and large companies upgrade their equipment every couple of years in order to meet the demands of a competitive marketplace. Some companies donate their used machinery to charity, but many offer it to employees or auction it off. Look in the classified ads for upcoming auctions.

Setting up your computer system is like decorating a room: take it one step at a time. If you can only afford the bare necessities, get those and add the finishing touches later. Involve your children in the process.

Once you have a basic system set up, here are some child-friendly activities to try:

COMPUTER FUN ON A BUDGET

Introduce your children to computers early on with colorful storybook software. The pages come alive on the screen, effectively combining the best of books and television. Check with your local computer reseller for a list of gently used titles. A few public libraries allow you to check out children's software or shareware, and you can also check with the public school to see if there are any available products to try out at home.

164 Encourage the artist in your child with one of the many available "art studio" software packages. Your child can write and illustrate his own children's book, design customized greeting cards, or simply "draw" and "color." Be sure to print your child's masterpieces for display and gift-giving. Most of these programs are affordable, but to save money contact the marketing department of children's art software companies (such as Disney and Crayola) and ask about becoming part of a test-market group; selected families are sent not-quite-ready-for-release software to test in their homes. Participants in these test-market groups are required to report back to the company with any problems, glitches, or hiccups in the programming.

Comfy Easy Keys educational software is a product designed to introduce very young children (with tiny fingers) to the marvels of a personal computer. Each software package comes with a keyboard overlay, which fits snugly over your existing computer keyboard. Prices range from $24.00 to $79.00 (the average price of Easy Keys is $29.95). Each software package is interactive and educational. For more information about this product, call 1-800-99COMFY, or write to the company at 305 Madison Avenue, Suite 1165, New York, NY 10165.

165 Sign up with America Online and check out the Kids Only section. There you'll find hours of fun activities for an affordable flat monthly fee. In the Kids Only section, you can download children's painting programs and help your child create computer art for display on the art pages. Together you can download fun games by clicking on Game Grabber, or enjoy games online (such as Cranial Crunch, Joke Book, or Kids Only Quest Test). Explore the user-friendly homework help section, and show your child how she can research topics online in *Compton's Encyclopedia.* Find out about the latest sports news and information together, and enjoy the photo gallery of sports stars. Help your child join one of the many clubs available to children, such as animals and pets, astronomy, collecting, computing, cooking, environment, games, magicians, music, pen pals, science fiction, sports, or writers.

166 Involve your children in planning your next vacation by visiting travel sites on the Internet. Both America Online and CompuServe have sites dedicated to travel and trip planning, providing information on just about any destination you choose. You'll find out about the local hot spots, discount packages, street maps (for some cities), consumer reviews, climate, and history, and get answers to the most-asked questions about the city or national park you'd like to visit. As an added benefit, you can find the lowest possible airfares and hotel rates, then book your reservations in seconds.

167 Plan a theme party and use your computer to design your own invitations, party favors, and decorations. Have the children pick a theme (such as a Hawaiian Luau) and decide what kinds of decorations you'll need. If you don't have a color printer, don't worry; just have the children color the invitations and decorations with water-based markers. Inexpensive publishing packages are available at discount stores nationwide, and for as little as $10 your family can enjoy hours of creative fun.

Moderate-Priced Computer Enjoyment

168 Encourage the writer in your child by helping him write and illustrate his own storybook with your family computer. There are several software packages to choose from, but ClarisWorks for Kids (Claris) is easy for even young children to use and is moderately priced. Again, if you don't have a color printer don't worry; your child can add color to his printed pages with water-based markers, colored pencils, or crayons. Once the storybook has been written, illustrated, designed, printed, and colored, you can easily bind it by using two sheets of card stock paper for the cover and artist-grade linen tape for the edge: place the pages of the book between the front and back covers, staple the book together, and cover the edges (including the staples) with tape.

169 Playing chess stimulates a child's mind and builds logical reasoning skills, but if you don't know how to play it yourself your computer can help. Teach yourself and your child to play chess using Chess Mates from Brainstorm. The company, based in Irvine, CA, also offers a fundraising kit for your child's school. Call the company at 1-888-777-8502 to find out how your child can develop cognitive mastery while helping her school and community.

170 Family computing is for the birds. Find out how by seeing, hearing, and gathering information about bird species in North America. With the click of a mouse, you can discover which bird you saw in your backyard last week and learn about its feeding, nesting, and breeding habits. Or you can listen to more than 1,200 bird songs and calls. In seconds, your child can find out how to attract more birds to your yard or patio. Expand your family's enjoyment: keep track of the birds you see and compare them with the information you glean from software programs and Internet birding sites. To learn more about current or popular Internet addresses and software titles, try the birding area on America Online (keyword: bird).

Birds of North America, Birder's Diary, **and *Audubon Birds for Mac* are three software selections for the naturalist family. These comprehensive CD-ROMs are being used at more than 260 schools, colleges, and universities; they are easy to use and entertaining for the whole family. For more information, write to Thayer Birding Software, P.O. Box 43243, Cincinnati, OH 45243, or call them at 1-800-865-2473.**

171 Learn a second language together via interactive entertainment designed for children. Power-Glide by Dr. Robert Blair and MUZZY by the BBC both offer instruction in French, German, and Spanish; MUZZY also offers an Italian program. For more information about Power-Glide, contact GBC Homeschool Discount Warehouse at 1-800-775-5422. Younger children might do better with MUZZY; write to Early Advantage, 25 Ford Road, Westport, CT 06880.

More Expensive but Thrilling Computer Fun

Everyone has a Web page these days, from television

and radio stations to your family doctor, so why not you? With a photo scanner and Web design software, your children (with adult help) can create a fun, flashy Web site on the Internet. Web Workshop (Vividus) is a child-friendly product; call 1-888-484-8438 to find out which stores sell it in your area. If you subscribe to America Online, type the keyword AOLPress for free software you can download to create a Web page. Any similar software package should walk you and your children through the entire process of developing your place on today's information superhighway.

A digital camera allows you and your children to capture and transmit "real time" photographs in seconds. These cameras cost upwards of $300 and can be difficult to use, but the results are amazing. If your friends and family members use an online service, your children can e-mail photo greeting cards, postcards, or virtual photo albums made from pictures taken by the digital camera. This technology is exploding fast, and it's also possible to upgrade your digital camera to video. You'll need a very powerful home computer to run the necessary software, and you can expect to spend as much as $4,000 for a system that includes all the bells and whistles (so this activity isn't for everyone), but with all of that equipment you can produce your own professional-looking documentaries.

Computer Literacy for Today and Tomorrow

What is computer literacy, and how can you help your child develop it when you're not sure you have it? First of all, computer literacy is an ongoing process. Technology changes so quickly that when a product hits the market, a new product will soon render it obsolete. There are, however, some basic levels of literacy:

- **Level One:** a beginner who turns to a computer for occasional entertainment, research, or practical use (such as writing letters, balancing a checkbook, etc.). This person knows how to turn on the computer, access and use a simple software program, save files, and shut down the system when done.
- **Level Two:** uses a computer more regularly and understands how to use one or two more-advanced software packages (such as word processing, desktop publishing, interactive games, etc.). This person sends and receives e-mail and is able to access the World Wide Web to do research.
- **Level Three:** uses a computer on a daily basis and can operate a wide range of software—perhaps even running a home-based business. This person actively uses all available technology (such as downloading information from online sources, uploading and transmitting files via e-mail, etc.) and is able to install simple hardware and software upgrades.
- **Level Four:** is comfortable not only with commercial programs but also can plug in shareware and other applications to solve problems or enhance projects. This person can pull together information from a wide variety of sources, plug it all in to one place, and improvise (programming, scripting, etc.) when necessary.
- **Level Five:** a master of computer literacy—comfortable with any and all aspects of personal computers, from installation and use to programming and development. This person can build a computer from purchased components, develop programs for specific needs, extend existing applications, and troubleshoot problems.

According to FutureKids, a worldwide franchised computer school, a child entering the seventh grade should be at Level Two in computer literacy. In our home, Dad is at Level Five, our older son is at Level Three, Mom is somewhere between Levels Two and Three, and our youngest—a beginner—has finally stopped banging the mouse on the desk. My point is that even if you're a little technologically challenged (as I am), you can give your children the opportunity to spend about forty-five minutes a week using the home computer. That's all it takes for them to gain the skills they need.

Making Your Way Through a Maze of Software Options

I've already shared a few tips on finding software that's suitable and affordable for your family, but to summarize:

- Check out the software programs available and accessible through the Kids Only site on America Online—all of which are free with your monthly flat-fee service charge

- Contact software companies that specialize in children's programs, and ask to have your family added to their test-market lists

- Don't forget that computer resellers offer gently used software packages for a fraction of the original price

- Contact your local public library to see if any software is available for checking out

Beyond those measures, how can you determine whether one program is "better" than another? How do you know what to look for? Are all children's software products "educational"? Which ones are appropriate for your children? Do they reinforce your family's values? How can you know what your children will be exposed to?

174 Read magazine reviews. *Child*, *Parenting Magazine*, *Parents*, and *Working Mother* magazines run monthly review columns that list the latest and greatest in software options for children. *Family PC* magazine is completely dedicated to family computing and abounds with reviews, activities, information, and help for any level of computer literacy. All of these publications are available at grocery stores, bookstores, and libraries.

175 Ask around: which software did the local school district purchase? Why did they purchase it? The answers will help you determine whether it's something you'd be interested in buying for your home. Don't forget to ask about ease of use; there is nothing more frustrating than struggling to understand a poorly designed software package.

176 Take a program for a test ride *before* your children see it. Companies that advertise in parent-oriented magazines sometimes offer demos that can be downloaded from a Web site. For example, LucasArts Entertainment Company will let you preview their Monkey Island software free of charge at their Web site (www.lucasarts.com). Take advantage of this option whenever possible and you'll know before you buy whether it's right for your child.

177 Get recommendations from homeschoolers—a resource that's too often overlooked. Parents who educate their children entirely at home know what children will or won't use, what's really educational, and whether a product is priced fairly. Homeschoolers can tell you which software is advertised as "educational"—but in practical use is little more than a game. They can tell you which programs might be too intense or frightening, and which ones are too dull. How do you find homeschoolers? Locally, you can contact the public library and see if there's a listing for your area. You can also contact the National Homeschool Association, P.O. Box 290, Hartland, MI 48353, for information about groups in your area (including the address or phone number for a local coordinator). Members of America Online can go to keyword homeschool, for access to hundreds of homeschooling families across North America.

Navigating the Internet and Making It Safe for Your Kids

What you've read in the newspaper and seen on the 5:00 news is true: lurking on every Internet Service Provider (ISP) are a few unstable, dangerous people—people who prey on children. It's hard enough to protect our children in our everyday lives, so how can we protect them from jeopardy in a medium we don't fully understand?

Some providers are making this task easier for parents by providing built-in controls to "lock" kids out of potentially dangerous areas. America Online leads ISPs in this effort, even employing adult decoys at the Kids Only site to patrol for would-be child molesters who pose as children.

Not all ISPs offer this kind of support, and once your child has accessed the World Wide Web there are no built-in controls. You can, however, purchase software specifically designed to make the Internet safe for your children to explore. One of the best products on the market is Cyber Patrol, by Microsystems Software. Two choices (cyberYES and cyberNOT) help you restrict certain areas according to their content. Filters are available in twelve categories and can be customized to your requirements. You can also prevent your children from attempting any research using sexually explicit terms. For more information, contact Microsystems Software: 1-800-489-2001.

Relatively new technology allows families to "surf the Net" without a computer. For about $300, you can purchase a specialized modem and keyboard that work with any television set, providing access to the World Wide Web. Again, there are no built-in controls on the Internet, and restrictive software is useless without standard computer equipment. Therefore, to keep your children away from explicit material, adult supervision is recommended.

All of that said, here's a list of safe, entertaining, "kid approved" sites that your children can investigate without worry:

- Animal Planet: www.animal.discovery.com
- Cyberkids: www.cyberkids.com
- Disney: www.disney.com
- 4Kids: www.4kids.com
- Lego: www.lego.com
- National Geographic OnLine: www.nationalgeographic.com
- Nickelodeon: www.nick.com
- Nye Labs (with Bill Nye, the Science Guy): www.nyelabs.com
- Scholastic Place: place.scholastic.com/index.htm
- *Sports Illustrated for Kids*: www.pathfinder.com

- The History Net: www.thehistorynet.com/home.html
- Yahoo! Headlines: www.yahoo.com/headlines
- Yahooligans: www.yahooligans.com
- Xplore Kids: www.xplore.com

CHAPTER

Historically Speaking

Your child's history is just that: *his* story. This includes not only an accounting of events in his life but important facts about the people most important to him today, as well as those who lived long ago.

Every Family Has a History—Mapping Yours

Every family has volumes of stories to tell. Some family tales remind us of a daytime soap, while others leave us rolling with laughter. A colorful family can supply a film writer with enough material to last an entire career.

That brings up the question: *Do I really want my children to know about the painful or complex issues in our past?* The answer depends on your own comfort level, the issues involved, and the ages of your children. Speaking from experience, even dysfunctional families hold enough happy memories to provide stories that will give your children a solid foundation. Mapping your background is worth the time and effort for a number of reasons:

- Magical moments creep into ordinary events, but recognizing them is an acquired skill. I hope this book has reminded you of some magical moments in your own childhood; sharing those memories gives your children a better glimpse of who you are.
- In our mobile society, we rarely have an opportunity to draw from the experiences of our older family members. We also miss out on important events in each other's lives. It's nice to reconnect with each other from time to time.
- Recording your combined history attaches new importance to the family unit; it immortalizes all of the players while bringing a fresh sense of appreciation for those you love.
- A few pleasant recollections can act as a balm for past or current injury. Happiness is a powerful healer. It can also take the fire out of ire. Our youngest child often brings me a special storybook when he's been scolded; he already knows that my annoyance will fade slowly as I read about the day he was born.
- Most people have little use for horse manure *unless* they're planting a rose garden; nothing else produces a better show of blooms. Likewise, negative experiences from your past can become empowering lessons for your children.
- Have you ever felt mired in the mud? Sometimes, in order to move ahead in the right direction, we have to look back to see where we've been—and how far we've already come.

There's no right or wrong way to map the history of your family. You can:

- Include as many people and events as you'd like, or as few

- Develop an elaborate collection of biographical information, or stick with highlights
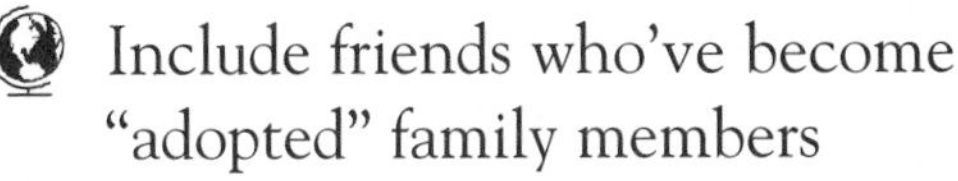
- Include friends who've become "adopted" family members
- Spend a lot of money gathering and putting information into a professionally edited and published book

- Simply fill in the blanks on a purchased "family tree" poster

> *"When you are getting kicked in the rear, it means you're in front."*
> —FULTON SHEEN

Most of us record important events on videos or in snapshots, creating a pictorial record of our lives and our children's lives. How you map your family history will be as individual as you are, but you can get started with a few easy ideas that incorporate photographs:

178 Create a family picture wall of portraits. Any busy parent knows that color portraits make wonderful, inexpensive, easy gifts at the holidays; if you don't already own a collection of photos, ask your family members for portraits. Include as many extended family members as possible. Dig out old photographs and frame them. Allow your picture wall to grow as your family grows; anyone visiting your home is sure to linger by that wall to uncover a bit of your history, and your children will enjoy sharing stories about their relatives.

179 Pull out a box of photos once or twice a year and have "family history" night. You can take advantage of the opportunity to reminisce with your children, and it's a fun way to organize individual photo albums using each child's favorite pictures.

180 Assemble a family collage. Purchase a medium to large picture frame that holds a mat with multiple picture openings. Gather a few stacks of photographs, and spread out a variety of children's stickers. Remove the mat board from the frame; count, with your children, the number of openings; and together search your snapshots for good pictures of each family member, including extended family. Fill each mat opening with a photograph of a different person. Ask your children to think about a character trait that best suits each family member, and place a symbolic sticker next to that person's photograph. For example: Papa Jay is generous with his time, attention, love, and possessions, so a sticker of a pot of gold would work. Grandma Audrey is kind and loving, so a sticker of a heart goes next to her picture. Papaw is wise (use a sticker of books), Mamaw is a good listener (use a sticker of an ear), and so on. When all the photographs and stickers are in place, reassemble the frame and hang your collage where you can see it—and talk about it—regularly.

> *"The virtue of the camera is not the power it has to transform the photographer into an artist, but the impulse it gives him to keep on looking."*
>
> —Brooks Atkinson

181 Photographs can also help with furniture refinishing; if your coffee table has seen better days, have a craft or hardware store cut a piece of glass (or Plexiglas) the same size as the top of your table and sand the edges smooth, then place photographs underneath the glass top. You can change the photographs from time to time, thus providing fresh faces and memories, and encouraging "historical" chats with your children.

182 Display your child's artwork gallery-style; expand this gallery as your child grows. Ask her to select a few favorite works once or twice a year. To save money, take advantage of advertised frame sales at art stores and frame shops. Be sure to select mat board that matches or accents each painting or drawing, choose a nice frame, date the back of each work, and hang the masterpieces on a dedicated wall or room in your home. When your child reaches adolescence, you'll have a colorful record of her growth—and you will have instilled an enduring interest in the arts.

183 Pictures aren't the only items that add color and ambiance to your home's decor; moderately priced shadow boxes are available through art supply catalogs, frame shops, and a few discount stores. A shadow box is essentially a frame that's deep enough to hold special treasures, such as ticket stubs, postcards, wedding invitations, award ribbons, small trinkets, or other memorabilia. By grouping an assortment of shadow boxes on a wall, you'll

> *"Every artist writes his own autobiography."*
> —HAVELOCK ELLIS

provide a silent history of good times for your children to reflect upon.

When you've filled your home with an illustrated history, you might want to polish your writing skills and try a few of the following ideas:

184 Enjoy a cross-country family game called Once Upon a Time. Extended family members and friends participate as players; each player is given a list of three people to contact and must develop three questions to ask the people about themselves. Next the players compose a letter to each of their three people, asking the three questions (similar to a chain letter). Small children can dictate their questions to an older child or adult. Any replies are photocopied and forwarded to the other players. This is a game in which more players mean greater learning, and it's a great way for your child to connect with the special people in his life.

185 Expand the scope of Once Upon a Time by starting a new Thanksgiving tradition: in September or October, have your children ask loved ones to write a special childhood memory on a sheet of notebook paper. Each child will also compose one page that describes a special experience (younger children can dictate to someone older). Include as many people as possible, and remember that out-of-town friends and relatives can mail their musings if they won't be attending your family's Thanksgiving festivities. Purchase a cloth-covered binder for your children to decorate with markers or paint; encourage a design that illustrates love, thankfulness, and family ties. Collect all of the written recollections in this notebook; add section dividers for each name or year if you'd like. Finally, as you polish off the last of the pumpkin pie, read the stories aloud together. It won't be long before your family has volumes of happy history to read and reread!

186 Our older relatives have so much to share with our children, and it's a shame that time or distance leave little opportunity for nostalgic storytelling. That's why some grandparents and great-grandparents look into publishing autobiographies; they're a way to pass a bit of themselves on to younger generations. My husband's grandmother is one of those aspiring writers; she eventually "published" a spiral-bound collection of stories, old photos, favorite songs, and prayerful poems called *Slices of My Life*. Using nothing more than a typewriter, any grandparent can create a priceless gift of history for your children. The typed pages (along with black-and-white photographs) can be copied, collated, and bound at any print shop. Ask your child's grandparents if they'd be willing to write an autobiography, and offer to help them "publish" it.

> *"History is Philosophy teaching by examples."*
>
> —HENRY ST. JOHN

187 Take advantage of computer software programs designed to help you track, collect, and record your ancestry. Family Tree Maker (Broderbund Software) sells for about $60 and is easy to use. Reunion (Leister Productions) is a more expensive option—it retails for $100—but is ideal for blended families. There are several other programs available, as well as Internet sites devoted to genealogy. Older children can help you find a software package (or technological assistance) that's both useful and user-friendly.

A Day at the Museum, or a Sunday Drive?

No matter where you live, a rich history surrounds you. There might be museums to explore, historical landmarks to visit, old houses to tour, national parks to romp in, or back roads to travel. You can spend many years of weekends exhausting all the possibilities with your children. Your city's Chamber of Commerce should offer a listing of popular places to investigate. Your state's Department of Tourism can fill in any blanks. Both of those resources provide information free of charge.

Your family can also enjoy spontaneous exploration. Let's say you wake up one Sunday morning feeling restless; you decide to load the children into the car and head out for the day with no specific destination in mind. Can an impromptu outing provide lessons in history?

Or perhaps it's been a long, draining week and you just want to cocoon at home. Can your children enjoy glimpses of the past without going anywhere?

Whether planned or improvised—and even without leaving your home—your children can brush up on history and have fun in the process. It's easier and cheaper than you might think. Beginning with a few traditional activities, think about ways your family can enjoy history on the weekends. For example:

The *Journal of Online Genealogy* is a monthly electronic magazine that offers tips and reviews for anyone interested in tracing family roots with the help of modern technology. To enjoy this publication, visit http://www.onlinegenealogy.com/.

188 Visit an art museum and examine works that were painted hundreds of years ago. Help your children compare artistic styles from one century to the next. Ask your child which style is his favorite. Encourage him to imagine the artist's daily life during the time of the painting (he can study the painting for clues): Where does he think the artist lived? What kind of clothes would the artist have worn? What kind of friends would stop by for a visit? What would be served for dinner? Of course, most paintings won't give you that depth of insight—but it's fun to imagine!

189 Spend an afternoon at a historical museum and encourage your children to explore with imagination. Don't just look at the artifacts under glass; think about the people who originally owned them or used them. If there are old photographs of your downtown area, point out the little details; visit the same spot and compare the differences. Talk about the things that appear to interest your child; encourage her questions and ask a few of your own.

190 Stroll through a sports museum to learn about the history of the game with your child. Linger in front of displays. Learn about favorite players. Talk about your own sports heroes, and ask about your child's. Memorize a few stats together. Hold an informal contest to see how many historical facts each child uncovers throughout the day.

191 Many communities host tours of historical homes during the holiday months, and the cost of these tours can vary from nothing to $8 per adult (children generally are admitted free of charge with an accompanying adult). Urge your child to ask questions on the tour. Point out interesting furnishings, fixtures, or photographs as you walk through each home. Wonder out loud what it would have been like to live in the houses during the era in which they were built.

192 Tour the birthplace of a historical hero with your children. What insights do the books, decorative items, toys, or trinkets provide? Ask your children to pretend they're doing research for a biography of the person, and see what they can uncover through subtle clues.

Here are a few less conventional ideas; some of these activities might surprise you!

193 Bring your children to a Renaissance Faire. Stroll through the crafts village, enjoy hundreds of costumed villagers, and sample the food and drink of bygone years.

194 Go antiquing together and—if possible—bring along an older relative. Your children will get to see "ancient" toys, books, and memorabilia, and your senior guest can provide information about items that were popular during his or her youth. Often simple items spark wonderful stories. Everyone can have fun, and this educational opportunity costs little more than lunch at a nearby sandwich shop.

195 When you're out for a weekend drive, watch for signs that advertise landmarks or tourist spots. If you're exploring a rural area, ask a gas station attendant or shop owner for recommended family stops. There may be a local restaurant that's been around for a few generations. The post office might hold some historical significance. When was the main church building erected? Can your family tour the church grounds?

196 Cemeteries aren't always creepy; they can be educational. You'll often find old cemeteries in small towns or rural areas, and chances are good that your children will think it's cool to visit one. As you stroll among the headstones and read the inscriptions, talk about what life was like during that period of time.

197 Ohio residents can "ride" the Underground Railroad with their children, and most "stops" are located in lush country areas. It's a wonderful way to learn about history and culture together. Are similar opportunities available in your area?

198 For an unusual and memorable weekend, pick an era and gather some library books to prepare for a one-day reenactment of history. Have your children make lists of the clothing, furnishings, toys, and popular activities for your chosen time period. Next, assign a date for your reenactment, mark it on the calendar and—as much as possible—gather or make outfits, toys, and other props so that the day will seem somewhat authentic. If there was no electricity during this time, buy some candles or dig out that camping lantern. Meals, of course, need to be prepared using modern appliances (or you can prepare the food in advance). From dawn until dusk on your chosen day, have the entire family pretend to be living during your chosen time period.

Here's a list of board games your children will love:

199 Experience life in the eighteenth century at your kitchen table with a board game called Catchpenny (Chatham Hill Games). Catchpenny is similar to the popular game Monopoly; players can buy, sell, and trade properties using Old English crowns, shillings, and pence. A bailiff and debtor's prison await the penniless player, and accumulation of wealth follows the life and customs of British monopolies during 1775 (complete with fun historical facts).

200 Another exciting board game by the same company is PiQadilly Circus (Chatham Hill Games). Adults and children compete on equal footing in this fast-paced game. Designed to teach word knowledge Victorian style, PiQadilly Circus combines history, vocabulary, strategy, and fun for everyone.

201 Take a trip to a nineteenth-century baseball field with 1876 Centennial Baseball (Chatham Hill Games). Your family will learn about the origins and history of baseball, fun facts, and early statistics as you compete in a real game the way it would have been played from 1860 through 1890; a booklet of original rules is included. This board game can be enjoyed long after baseball season has ended.

202 When chilly November days keep you inside on the weekend, prepare for Thanksgiving fun with The Voyage Of The Mayflower (Chatham Hill Games). This board game gives your children the opportunity to sail across the stormy Atlantic with the Pilgrims as they make their way to America. It's a fun and exciting game that's loaded with educational information; it provides unique entertainment at Thanksgiving or throughout the year.

203 Unplug the Nintendo controls and set up Gettysburg: The Battlefield Game (Chatham Hill Games) on your kitchen table; any child who loves war games will enjoy this one. Union and Confederate players face off using knowledge and luck; the game can be played with or without the more than 160 questions provided. Involve your entire family, and everyone will become an expert in the Battle of Gettysburg.

204 Masterpiece (Parker Brothers) is an art history board game that's available anywhere children's games are sold. Retailing for about $15, this game uses picture cards of well-known paintings that are available for "auction." It's a great way to expand your study of history to include art and culture worldwide.

Catchpenny, PiQadilly Circus, 1876 Centennial Baseball, The Voyage Of The Mayflower, and Gettysburg: The Battlefield Game are all available through Chatham Hill Games, Inc., P.O. Box 253, Chatham, NY 12037, 1-800-554-3039, or CHGames@taconic.net. These board games sell for $29.95 each and are well worth the price. Chatham Hill also offers low-cost board games for history buffs. At $7 each, the games offer affordable fun and learning; there are fifteen topics to choose from. You can also purchase inexpensive historical maps or a family tree poster from Chatham Hill.

Learning About History the Easy Way—Together

So far we've uncovered ways to share your family heritage, experience local history, and explore special periods, topics, or events—all of which develop basic interests, skills, and knowledge. When your children begin a more formal study of history in school, they'll have an edge because of the fun learning they've experienced at home.

You'll want to continue the process in greater depth as your children grow. Why? Well, think about it: how exciting were *your* history classes? Sure, the field trips were enjoyable—if only because they took you away from the classroom for a day—but did you otherwise enjoy United States history as it was taught in school? What about world history? Were your textbooks entertaining, or were they thick volumes of tedious names, dates, facts, and timelines?

Schoolbooks have come a long way since we nodded off in history class, and there are countless other books you can enjoy reading with your children: entire collections of biographies, historical novels, storybooks, and titles you'd never associate with history.

Historical information lurks in many unlikely books and magazines. For example, is your child fascinated with special effects or camera tricks? Older issues of *TV Guide* and photography journals might provide background information (check with your library for availability of back issues). Pick up a library book about filmmaking to share with your child; most will give a brief history of the field. To uncover history in just about any interest or hobby, look for interesting articles or books that provide information about its beginnings. In fact, you can refresh your own knowledge and enjoy time together with surprisingly little effort. Through family reading, games, crafts, and play, your children will be soaking up even more education. *Shhh! Don't tell them!*

205 Search used-book stores for a series called *Cornerstones of Freedom*. The series was published in the 1970s for intermediate readers (ages eight to twelve), but with fewer than thirty-five pages of text and several illustrations in each book, younger children can benefit, too—especially if you're reading to them. My sister passed down her son's collection of thirty-four titles to my children, and even our youngest enjoys the books. I prefer the older, hardcover editions, but a recent paperback series is also available for about $4 per book.

206 Chelsea House Publishers supplies public schools and libraries with hundreds of educational titles. You can purchase paperback versions of easy-to-read collections, such as *American Women of Achievement* (twelve titles), or *Discovering America* (seventeen titles). Other series are available in a variety of topics. For more information, or to request a catalog, contact Chelsea House at 1-800-848-BOOK.

207 Check with your public library to find a few issues of *American History* magazine. The publication is thoughtful and entertaining. Although it's geared to a more advanced reader, your children might enjoy the vivid articles and colorful artwork. Page through an issue with them; if they seem interested, try a one-year subscription. Read the articles together and encourage your children to ask questions about topics they don't understand. You can subscribe to *American History* through America Online's electronic newsstand services.

208 Speaking of magazines with family appeal, consider a subscription and membership to *Smithsonian*. For about $24, you'll receive twelve issues of the magazine, discounts on all Smithsonian catalog purchases, special savings through the museum gift shops, a dining discount at The Wright Place Restaurant, free admission to the Cooper Hewitt National Design Museum in New York City, members-only travel options, and a personalized membership card. I'll bet you didn't realize $24 could go that far toward your child's education! For subscription information, write to Smithsonian, P.O. Box 420319, Palm Coast, FL 32142.

209 If you have a school-aged daughter, you may already know about the *American Girl* series; if you don't, look for the books in the children's section of your local bookstore. Titles are available in both hardcover and paperback. There are paper dolls and large vinyl dolls that accompany the series, and your daughter can join the American Girls club or visit the American Girls site on the Internet. Thousands of little girls (and their parents) are learning about United States history through this popular series.

A $20 subscription to the American Girls Club includes a year's worth of magazines, the American Girls Handbook, a bi-monthly newsletter, and enough projects to keep your daughter entertained indefinitely. Keep in mind that, although the main characters are little girls, some boys figure into the story line in prominent ways, and sons can participate in many of the suggested activities, such as making quill pens from turkey feathers and ink from walnuts, preparing meals from the cook-book, or putting on a historical play with Colonial costumes.

210 The *Little House on the Prairie* books by Laura Ingalls Wilder are another avenue for entertainment and learning. You can find these paperbacks in any major bookstore. When you read them aloud by a crackling fire on a cold

winter evening, the whole family will warm up to American history. When you've exhausted the series, look for books by Jean Fritz at your local public library; they'll provide additional information and entertainment.

211 Rent or purchase cassette tapes of celebrated folk songs or ballads from long ago and sing along with your children when you're stuck in traffic. Some tapes come with songbooks that include information about the tunes and the history behind them. Most public libraries have collections of videos and cassettes that you can check out for a few days or weeks, allowing for unlimited sing-along fun.

212 Learn about American folk art and early American crafts through books, magazines, or videotapes. When you find a craft that is of special interest to your children, take up the hobby together. Spinning, weaving, or candle-making as a family can be a great way to learn about Colonial life. Whittling together can provide an education in post-Revolutionary history. Tole painting offers an understanding of Dutch immigrants. In fact, every American craft has historical ties that can bring your family closer together as you gain knowledge and skills.

I've been blessed with countless opportunities to explore the United States during family vacations and (too many) cross-country moves. In thirty-six years, I've visited our nation's capital more times than I can count, and I've experienced everything from secluded barns to overcrowded cities, flat plains to snowcapped mountains, parched desserts to the Great Lakes, and southern plantations to New York subways. In fact, I've zigzagged from the Atlantic to the Pacific and back again at least three times.

As a child, history came alive for me during our travels in a way that it never did in the classroom. I loved to imagine myself living among the people of the past, my footsteps falling where they once walked. I feel the same way today. The following suggestions should tempt you to explore America's history firsthand with your children:

213 Plan a vacation to Williamsburg, Virginia, and your family will witness Colonial life on a grand scale. The surrounding area is rich in history as well: Jamestown is a few miles down the freeway; Monticello, Arlington, and Washington, D.C., are about three hours north by car (you can stop in Richmond on your way and stroll through a Confederate museum); and the Wright Brothers' Museum in Kitty Hawk is three to four hours south. In other words, you can pack several years' worth of history classes into a week or two of family fun. If you'd like to plan a vacation that begins in Williamsburg, call 1-800-311-6361 and ask for the Williamsburg Vacation Package brochure.

Victorian Video Productions offers a multitude of "how-to" videos relating to heritage handicrafts. Your family can learn about lace-making, spinning, weaving, needlework, embroidery, knitting, crocheting, fabric painting, basketry, appliqué, beadwork, and more. There are 175 titles to choose from. Each instructional video explores not only techniques but the history behind each hobby. Write to Victorian Video Productions, Inc., P.O. Box 1540, Colfax, CA 95713, or call them at 1-800-848-0284.

214 Visit a few of the many "living museums" in Massachusetts during late autumn and experience the day-to-day lives of America's pilgrims. Children and history buffs will love sauntering through historical villages in Deerfield, Plymouth, and Sturbridge. "Interpreters" dressed in period costumes plant the fields, chop wood, spin wool, weave cloth, tend to sewing, and act out other daily chores while answering visitors' questions. For $100 per plate, your family can partake of original Pilgrim fare during a reenactment of the first Thanksgiving. For much less money, your children can tour a cider mill, tin shop, copper shop, pottery barn, or busy plantation. These villages prove that learning can be fun; even the trendiest of children will be fascinated and educated during your visit.

215 Next time you're going to Boston, Philadelphia, or New York on business, bring the family along. Each of these cities holds more historical attractions than I could possibly list. In fact, during one extended weekend of sightseeing, your children will learn more than any history book could teach them—and so will you!

216 Remember the Alamo? Texans are proud of their heritage, and the entire state welcomes tourists. There's plenty to see and do in Texas, but you'll definitely want to take your young cowpokes through Austin, Dallas, Fort Worth, and San Antonio for a well-rounded lesson in the history of the Southwest.

217 Do you yearn for warm sand, snowy peaks, abundant orchards, and towering forests? You can find all of that and more in a single state: California. More than sunny beaches and crowded cities, a week there can provide your family with many adventures in history as you make your way from the redwood forests to San Diego's marina. The Pacific Coast Highway is spectacular any time of year, with places of interest—including Hearst Castle—sprinkled along the way.

218 Speaking of the Pacific coast, your family can cruise along the Lewis & Clark Trail, the Oregon Trail, and the Columbia River Gorge, soaking up history along the way. To plan your cruise, write to the American West Steamboat Company, 601 Union Street, Suite 4343, Seattle, WA 98101, and ask for a free brochure.

219 Ride the Grand Canyon Railway together and enjoy Western characters, strolling musicians, and canyon rim tours as you relive the excitement of the Wild West. Not only is this fun for everyone, it's more affordable than you might think. Call 1-800-THE-TRAIN for information and a trip-planning package.

220 Experience the annual Fall Pilgrimage in Natchez, Mississippi and stay for the Great Mississippi Balloon Race (the dates of the events overlap). Located on the Mississippi River, Natchez is the state's historic gem, offering countless opportunities for family fun and learning. You can contact the Natchez Convention and Visitor's Bureau for more information by calling 1-800-99-NATCHEZ. Or, if you're a fan of Mark Twain and you enjoy military memorabilia, spend a few days in Vicksburg; your family can enjoy a multitude of museums, historic home tours, and riverboat excursions. To plan your trip, call 1-800-221-3536.

221 The heartland is home to a rich heritage of Americana. From the Amish countryside, through miles of farmland, into cityscapes with a hometown feel, you and your children will understand why the Midwest is integral to the story of the United States. You also won't find a more family-friendly area on earth. Pick up a copy of *Midwest Living* magazine, and you'll find an abundance of travel information—including vacations off the beaten path.

I know I've left out a lot of wonderful places, but you get the idea: *begin with your own state and discover as much of America as you can with your children*. Not only will they be educationally enriched but the memories of a special vacation will linger in their hearts and minds for a lifetime.

Would a Video Be a Good Idea?

Admittedly, not everyone has the time or money to travel coast to coast in an effort to teach their children about our country and its history. Many families have a bonafide family vacation only a few times a decade—often spent visiting relatives.

When your budget and schedule don't allow for an extended trip, it's possible to travel America and learn about history through videos. You may be wondering, "Are there any historical videos that are entertaining?" Yes. Would your family gain anything by watching them? Well . . . haven't you enjoyed television shows about places of interest in the United States? Or the history of airplanes? Or World War II? Do you enjoy movies that are set in another time?

A lot of parents worry that their children already watch too much television. In some households videos aren't encouraged, but in others they're a favorite diversion. If you're concerned yet undecided, remember that videos don't have to *replace* all other forms of entertainment. You've provided your children with an environment rich in educational opportunities through books, games, and other explorations, and videos can be a wonderful supplement to the learning experience. Here are a few you'll enjoy with your children:

222 Learn about literature, history, and basic values with an adorable pooch named Wishbone. Manufactured and marketed by PolyGram Video, each tape includes two episodes from the popular PBS television series. Check your cable listings, too, because many public television stations offer the Wishbone series during after-school hours.

223 Another popular PBS show that's available on video is the *Anne of Green Gables* series. Each episode provides warm, sometimes funny glimpses into the past. Your public library may offer the videos in this series for rent, or you can ask about them at any video store.

224 While you're whipping up dinner one evening, tune in to *Where in Time Is Carmen Sandiego?* on your local PBS channel. This fast-paced game show thrills even young children. During membership drives, video collections of Carmen Sandiego episodes are often available for sale (proceeds go to support your public television station).

225 Adolescents will enjoy watching *Biography* (Arts & Entertainment channel), *Intimate Portrait* (Lifetime channel), or *In Search of History* (History channel); each of these popular shows is available on video. Rent or purchase them from a well-stocked video store—such as Blockbuster Video—or order them directly via television advertisements.

226 Your children can become experts on North American Indian tribes, from the Apaches through the Yankton Sioux, through individual videos in Chelsea House Publisher's *Indians of North America* collections. Although these thirty-minute videos aren't cheap ($39.95 each or $399.50 per collection of ten), your family can gain a deeper understanding of the history, culture, and contributions of Native Americans while munching popcorn in front of the TV. Your public library may stock the videos, or call 1-800-848-BOOK for more information.

227 GCB's catalog offers a number of historical videos from an evangelical Christian perspective, as well as a collection of C. S. Lewis titles (from the popular BBC series). Affordably priced, these videos offer wholesome entertainment for everyone. Although some of the historical videos inject a strong political viewpoint into chronological facts (and the expressed views might not agree with yours), the catalog descriptions are detailed enough to allow for careful selection. Check large local churches with well-stocked libraries, or call 1-800-775-5477 for more information and a free catalog.

What about learning history through art? There

A*rt and Civilization,* a comprehensive book by well-known art historian and critic Edward Lucie-Smith, is a wonderful addition to any home library and builds upon any art video series. The 560-page edition—though not "light" reading—includes 555 illustrations, timelines, and maps. Look for it at any major book store, or order it through Dick Blick Art Materials, 1-800-447-8192.

are a number of excellent art history videos, including a new collection based on another BBC series, *Sister Wendy's Story of Painting* (available through your local public television station). Your children can learn about world history through any video or series that explores significant periods in art, music, literature, and philosophy.

CHAPTER

Other Places, Other Cultures

Do you remember *The Ed Sullivan Show? Dragnet? Flipper? The Partridge Family?* It used to be that television's sole purpose was to entertain the masses in the comfort of their well-worn recliners. When the dinner dishes were dried and stacked, families gathered in front of large, glowing boxes to unwind at the end of a busy day. Children sprawled out on shag carpeting, shushing each other during the exciting parts, and Dad sometimes fell asleep before the show ended.

I was in grade school when all of that changed; educational television was born through children's shows such as *Romper Room* and *Captain Kangaroo*. Those popular programs were soon followed by *Sesame Street* and *Mister Rogers' Neighborhood*. Then we were introduced to *Reading Rainbow*—and a slew of other shows—which proved that television could be fun *and* enlightening. Elementary schools brought televisions into the classroom as a supplement for textbook studies, and we expanded the way we look at learning. In as little as thirty minutes—and while being entertained—students can soak up information and experience learning.

> *"All television is educational television. The question is: what is it teaching?"*
>
> —NICHOLAS JOHNSON

The Success of Geography Programs on Television

Because I believe that children learn more when they're having fun, I understand the success of geography programs on television. Public television allows your child to voyage across the Pacific on a Kon-Tiki or stroll the streets of London. Sure, he can read about those places, but would he? Maybe, maybe not. It would depend on the books available to him and whether he found them interesting. A television show, on the other hand, might spark unexpected fascination—and learning!

For tonight's entertainment, round up your children, sink into your recliner, and watch one of the following television shows—then expand your family's learning experience long after the credits have rolled with the included tips and ideas:

229 National Geographic's *Really Wild Animals* isn't only about animals (although that's the main focus); it's a funky program that zips across the globe in search of fun facts, with the help of an animated host named Spin. Your children are sure to enjoy it. They can continue learning with Really Wild Animals: Swinging Safari (National Geographic), an interactive CD-ROM computer game. The software also acts as a desktop publishing program, helping your children produce cards, comic strips, letters, postcards, magazine articles, and newspapers.

230 *National Geographic Explorer* is excellent for children (and grown ups) of all ages. Each episode investigates one or two areas of the United States or the world at large, delving deeply into regional highlights and wonders. For example, recent episodes have taken viewers to the Andes mountains and the bat caves in Texas. The series can act as a springboard for family fun and learning; a subscription to *National Geographic* magazine provides colorful maps of the explored areas, and *National Geographic World* magazine (for children) supplies easy-to-read articles that pick up where the show left off.

231 *World of National Geographic* examines various regions more completely, integrating history, ecology, and politics through an engaging format that appeals to children and adults. Your family will learn about many places and cultures, and you can follow up with library books, puzzles, ethnic recipes, or other ideas afterwards.

Sign your child up for a National Geographic Junior Membership ($17.95), which includes a one-year subscription to *World* magazine. Write to National Geographic Society, P.O. Box 64066, Tampa, FL 33664-4066, or call 1-800-NGS-LINE. You can also subscribe on the Internet by visiting www.nationalgeographic.com/kids.

2 3 2 *Adventurers* is an exciting show that touches on geography while highlighting the curiosity, inventiveness, and grit of special people who've dared to be different. It's rated for family viewing, but very young children may be frightened during a few dramatic scenes. Your school-aged children will love it, however. Because of the nature of this program, you'll have the opportunity to discuss the diversity of places *and* people with your children. It's a great lesson in the rewards of self-challenge; encourage your children to challenge themselves in smaller ways in school and on the home front.

2 3 3 *Castle Ghosts* is an annual PBS series that tours famous castles throughout Great Britain and Europe. Preteens will love the spookier elements of the show. Your entire family can learn a lot by expanding your viewing time to include travel shows—such as *Great Castles of Europe*—or historical dramas. You might also incorporate library books into your study of legendary castles and European lore.

2 3 4 Michael Palin (of *Monty Python* fame) will have you on the floor laughing with his PBS series, *Full Circle with Michael Palin*. His previous geography series (which are often shown in reruns) include *Around the World in 80 Days* and *Pole to Pole*. From the rainforests of Borneo to sheep farms on the coast of New Zealand, whether crossing the Nile or bargaining on the streets of Baghdad, Palin's unique brand of humor will hold your child's interest. Some of the humor might be inappropriate for very young children, so parents should preview an episode to establish a comfort-level rating. If you decide it's suitable for your family, pull a few encyclopedias off the shelf and follow along with your host as he circles the globe.

2 3 5 *New Explorers* is an Arts & Entertainment Channel program similar to *Adventurers*, but with a bit more "meat" and a little less drama. This is a great series for any family to enjoy together; young and old alike will love it, and hard-to-please adolescents will think it's cool. Place a globe on the coffee table so everyone can follow the geographical expeditions. Some of the episodes focus more on science and technology, so you might want to grab a dictionary or encyclopedia for those. Either way, the educational benefits are impressive.

Travel the World from Your Kitchen Table

If you criss-cross the globe, no matter where you pause there is one enduring symbol of family life: a table. In every country and every culture, families gather to share meals at a table. The foods we eat differ; the clothes we wear vary; our traditions, preparations, and practices are diverse; yet we all gather our families at a table for mealtime. *Your* kitchen table can become a pathway to the world.

Does that sound a little crazy? Improbable? Then you're in for some surprises, because each of the following activities involves your family's mealtime gathering place.

> *"When you're safe at home you wish you were having an adventure; when you're having an adventure you wish you were safe at home."*
>
> —THORNTON WILDER

AGES THREE TO FIVE

Preschoolers can be introduced to world geography during what I call "the whining hour"—that time of day when Daddy isn't home yet; everyone is tired, hungry, and cranky; and you're trying to throw something together for dinner. They'll be occupied, they'll develop critical fine-motor skills, and you'll have a few relatively quiet moments at the stove when you try these activities:

236 Begin with chunky crayons and an assortment of coloring books from Rand McNally Kids; these delightful (and inexpensive) coloring books can be found nationwide at any toy store, discount department store, bookstore, or teacher's resource shop. If relatives like to give your children coloring books as gifts, ask for the Rand McNally Kids coloring books by name. Collect several, and you'll have more than a month's worth of fun and learning.

237 Make large "play maps" to fit the top of your kitchen table by "laminating" inexpensive maps with clear vinyl adhesive paper. Simply lay each map flat, face down. Then cut sheets of the vinyl to size and press the sticky side to the map backs. Turn the maps over and repeat the process with the front sides. Gather a few Matchbox (Mattel) or Hot Wheels (Mattel) cars, give them to your preschoolers, and let them race their cars across the play maps. Your children will dissolve into giggles as the cars fly off of the tabletop, and you'll get at least twenty minutes of dinner-prep time while they play.

238 You can also make "place maps" in the same way by "laminating" maps that have been cut down to place mat size. Because the vinyl wipes clean, the place maps should last several months. Try giving your children bits of finger food that's placed directly on each place map during snack time and you'll never know how much geography they wind up absorbing with their apple slices.

239 For children who are around kindergarten age, invest $15 in Dorling Kindersley's World Explorer Activity Pack. Available wherever children's books are sold, this unique kit contains a child-friendly information book, activity book, jigsaw puzzle, stickers, poster, and picture postcards. Your little explorer is sure to get many evenings of fun, and you'll have the satisfaction of knowing that she's learning new skills while you're stirring the stew.

Ages Six to Ten

Children in this age group are exploding with growth. Their minds are also maturing, and they're curious about other people in the world. Together, you can launch a worldwide tour, experiencing places, people, and cultures. For each of the following ideas you'll need a calendar, an atlas (or book about geography), a set of encyclopedias, a willingness to try new recipes, and a spirit of adventure. Your mission is to circle the globe in one year.

240 On January 26, you'll begin in Australia. Your child should look up Australia in both the atlas and the encyclopedia, and you'll read about the country together. January 26 is the day when British prisoners arrived on the continent's shore. To commemorate the event, you'll be grilling shrimp on the "barbie" (or, if you live in a snowy area, in the oven), sampling a tossed fruit salad, and washing your dinner down with tea.

241 February 6 brings you to New Zealand to celebrate their national holiday. Again, you'll read about the country—but you'll also want to read about the Maori people, who were the original island dwellers. Tonight's feast will consist of roasted lamb, kiwi salad, and sparkling water.

242 Heading north, February 11 brings you to National Day in Japan. Everyone should come to the table wearing brightly colored clothes; make a special tablecloth by "painting" a red circle in the center of an old white sheet with permanent markers. Read about the country together and see if your children can find the name of the first emperor. Dinner will be easy tonight: stir-fry thin strips of beef or chicken with an assortment of fresh vegetables. Enjoy hot tea after your family meal.

243 If it's March 1, it must be Wales! Tonight you'll celebrate St. David's Day together. To do so, you'll need a bouquet of daffodils. Look up Wales together in your reference books, and prepare a meal of leek soup, roast beef, and bread pudding. If you have Celtic harp CDs or cassettes, play that music during your dinner hour. Following the meal, read about St. David, the patron saint of Wales.

244 Travel south to Greece for Independence Day on March 25. Play folk music as you read about this country; you may also want to try some of the folk dances! For a variety of recipe choices tonight, page through Jeff Smith's *Frugal Gourmet Cooks the Ancient Cuisines* (available at any public library) and pick a few things that fit your family's taste buds. After dinner, share a library book (or rented video) about Ancient Greece.

245 April 30th's celebration takes place in the Netherlands, where the entire country is honoring their queen. As you read about the country, see what information your children can find about past and current royalty. Then—*your children will love this*—you'll all need to paint your faces orange (the official color of the Dutch Royal family) in honor of the holiday! Pop in some lively fiddling music, place a cluster of fresh tulips on the table, and enjoy a meal of boiled cod, fresh cheese, and green salad.

246 After a brief pause in your travels, June 2 brings you to Italy. In addition to reading about the country, you may want to rent a few videos about Florence (home of the Renaissance), Michelangelo and the Sistine Chapel, or Leonardo da Vinci for after-dinner viewing. A simple meal of pasta with sauce, salad, and bread should leave plenty of time to ponder the wealth of information available about Italy.

247 Cross the Atlantic to Canada on July 1, and ask your children to make place mats that resemble the country's flag (using construction paper and markers). Because there are so many provinces in Canada, it would take most of the night to make your way through an encyclopedia's survey of the country; try a library book instead or pick one province to read about. Enlist your children's help in preparing a dinner of their choice tonight (Canadian cuisine is similar to American cuisine). And for dessert? Vanilla ice cream with maple syrup topping!

248 The 4th of July takes you back home for a much-needed rest, and you'll want to incorporate as much U.S. history as you can into this year's celebration.

249 Back on the road—so to speak—you arrive in Bolivia on August 6. Buy several pieces each of red, yellow, and green felt, and have your children make Bolivian flags by gluing felt strips together and attaching them to small sticks or dowels. Read about the country and ask your children to locate the capital. Prepare a vegetarian meal tonight with seasoned steamed vegetables, fresh fruits, rice, and corn. Afterward, hold a family parade; march around the house and wave your flags proudly.

250 The tropical islands of Indonesia will be your stopping place on August 17. See if your children can name each island, major agricultural products, or interesting trivia about Indonesia. Keep the kitchen cool tonight by preparing a large fruit salad (using a few tropical fruits) and fruit smoothies to drink (using frozen fruit, skim milk, and a touch of sugar).

251 September 16 is Mexican Independence Day. Enjoy a meal out at your favorite Mexican restaurant and read about the country's rich heritage afterward. You may want to include a video about Mayan culture or construct a miniature temple out of cardboard—decorated with pen-and-ink glyphs.

252 Travel to Russia on November 7, and read about the Revolution of 1917. See how many different geographic areas your children can find on a map of the country. For example, do they know where Siberia is? Ask an older child to calculate the number of square miles in the country, and compare that number to the estimated square miles in the United States. Serve roasted meat (any kind) and lots of potatoes for dinner tonight. Keep in mind that most people living in that country have few choices in fresh produce, so skip the salad; steam a vegetable (like carrots or brussels sprouts) instead.

253 Tanzania's National Day falls on December 9. Since the year is winding up, go all out and create native headgear for each of your children to wear at dinnertime. You'll need paper plates, tempera paints, craft feathers, and string. Cut the bottom third off of each plate, and have your children carefully cut the center circle from the rippled edge of each plate. They'll paint that edge with bright tempera and, when the paint is dry, glue feathers onto the painted rim (pointing upward) in a plume. Finally, attach a string to the bottom edge of each side and tie the ends under each child's chin. Read about Tanzania together, then look up Julius Nyerere. Since native Tanzanians are expert hunters, roast Cornish game hens for dinner tonight.

254 It's January 26 again, and you're ending the year in India. Have a grand celebration tonight! Place a toy elephant in the center of your table as a centerpiece. Wrap turbans around the heads of the males in your family, and ask your children to make a red dot in the center of the forehead of each female. Place peeled, diced potatoes in a large pot, add 1 cup of plain yogurt, ½ cup of water, 1 teaspoon of curry powder, and a dash of salt and pepper; stir and cook over low heat while you read about the country (anywhere from thirty minutes to an hour). Steam (or microwave) several other vegetables, including carrots with honey and cinnamon, cabbage with lemon basil and cracked pepper, and assorted beans with fennel seed, garlic, and salt. After dinner, help each of your children make friendship bracelets (by braiding embroidery thread or yarn), and toast each other with sparkling cider for a year well spent!

Ages Eleven and Up

Older children and teens want to delve more deeply into topics and issues; their thought patterns are more "grown-up" and they are serious about life. This is an age when they demand more responsibility, and when you'll often hear the words "Stop treating me like a child!"

This is also a good time to expand the scope of your children's learning environment; introduce them to the world through a more powerful lens with some of these ideas:

255 Give your child a subscription to *The World & I* magazine. Published by The Washington Times Corporation, it's a serious periodical with an educated view of the arts, life, geography, history, science, economics, politics, culture, modern thought, literature, and more. It's also a magazine that opens the door for lively family discussions. A $45 subscription includes twelve issues and a monthly teacher's guide (the magazine is popular with middle schools and high schools). The teacher's guide is a useful way for parents to ask questions that spark communication. For more information, call 1-800-822-2822.

256 Stop by a few travel agencies and gather free brochures about a wide assortment of countries; spread them out on the table and review them together. Dream about a family vacation-of-a-lifetime. Brainstorm together and see if you can think of ways to save money to fund your trip. Consider pooling everyone's money in a group effort. It may take years to save for such a trip, but by involving your adolescent you're teaching valuable lessons that go beyond geography.

257 Encourage your older child to correspond with a foreign pen pal. This can be done via e-mail or the old-fashioned way, with the help of your child's school, church, synagogue, or language club.

258 Expand that thought and consider taking in a foreign exchange student. Check with your school district for more information about such programs. Younger children will benefit from this as well, and it's an enriching experience for everyone—often producing lifelong friendships.

259 Is your church or synagogue involved with mission programs? Sometimes youth groups organize annual "work holidays": participating teens travel to a mission field and help build or repair property with plenty of adult supervision. Ask for information or brochures and review them with your family.

Puzzled About Europe or the Middle East? Try a Puzzle!

Memorization has never been easy for me, and geography was sometimes daunting; I wasn't sure I could pronounce many of the names, let alone memorize them! Books were useful, and maps sometimes helped, but when it came to filling in the blanks, my mind generally went blank.

I was nearly thirty years old when our oldest son showed me an easier way: puzzles! My sister bought him an inexpensive wooden jigsaw puzzle of the United States for his third birthday, because (as she told me) he was "at the age" for beginning to play with puzzles. During the next year, he often dumped various puzzle pieces onto the floor and quietly reassembled them. I didn't think much of it—appreciating the brief respite from noise and dirt—until one day when he called out the name of each state as he put the pieces in place. In less than a year, he had learned the name of each state *and* the capital cities!

Jigsaw puzzles are ideally suited to family fun; you and your children can reap many hours of enjoyment piecing together—and *learning*—geography. Start with some of these, which are widely available wherever toys are sold:

- National Geographic Society puzzles range in price from about $2 to $5, and have as few as sixty pieces (ideal for small children) or as many as one thousand pieces (challenging for older children).

- Milton Bradley Company sells a line of puzzles called Little Big Ben, which sell for about $3. You'll find many European cities, parks, and tourist spots depicted in these puzzles.

- Dare your family with Puzz3D mini-puzzles ($5) or Super Challenge puzzles ($30) and build three-dimensional replicas of the Eiffel Tower, Big Ben, Notre Dame Cathedral, or other monuments and notable buildings.

If your family decides that puzzles are the perfect post-dinner pastime, consider additional options for family entertainment, including making your own puzzles. It's easier than you might think, even if you're artistically challenged.

260 Young children can quickly and easily cut up your "laminated" maps (with blunt-end scissors), creating their own jigsaw puzzles. They'll love the fact that they're being allowed to destroy something, and they'll feel important because they're making something for the family to enjoy. Children from the age of about five and up can carefully cut out each country, but younger children will probably cut at will (perhaps dissecting a country or two along the way); encourage creativity.

261 Combining aspects of flash cards with the Trivial Pursuit (Hasbro) board game, Geography Brain Quest (University Games) is a set of question-and-answer cards that can help your children develop another kind of puzzle: crossword puzzles! As with other Brain Quest packages, the cards retail for about $10. Older children can use the questions to develop their own crossword puzzle books, which will be used by the entire family game-show style. Once the puzzles are composed, set a timer on your kitchen table, assemble everyone (even young children), and take turns (one question at a time) filling in the first puzzle. Set a time limit for each player; when the timer rings, it's the next person's turn to answer. Unanswered questions can be looked up and filled in via the original set of Geography Brain Quest cards.

262 Using a Rand McNally Kids coloring book, run photocopies of a few maps. Apply correction fluid over the names of countries (for young children) or cities (for older children) and run another copy of each map. Your resulting puzzle maps will have blank spaces. Purchase a package of small white price labels and write the names of the "missing" countries or cities on them. Place your "puzzle" material and a kitchen timer on the table; have a children's atlas available. The object of this puzzle game is to place the appropriate stickers on the maps as quickly as possible. Have your children select a map, set the timer for five minutes, and GO! Repeat this process with as many maps as you have the energy to "solve." Encourage younger children to participate by assisting them as necessary; there are no winners or losers in this game.

263 Pretend to be traveling abroad and make jigsaw postcards to send to family and friends. You'll need a

Create-a-Puzzle package of twelve blank jigsaw puzzles (available at most art, craft, or hobby stores for about $3.50), colorful markers, an atlas, and a sense of humor. Ask your children to flip through the atlas and pick a vacation spot. Then have them draw and color a design that illustrates their choice. They can reproduce a map of the country, draw a picture of a landmark, design a baggage stamp, or whatever else suits their fancy. When the tops of the puzzles have been embellished, flip them over and ask your children to write a message on the back (postcard style). Then disassemble the puzzles, put the pieces into envelopes, and mail them off.

264 Create a trip puzzle and become tour guides. Spread out a large map of Europe, South America, Canada, or the Middle East on your table. Pass out a handful of water-based markers. Take turns being "leader"—a parent is the first leader and assigns a starting point. Slowly and carefully give a verbal "tour schedule" to each child, one player at a time so that everyone can share in the learning. For example, you might start in London and ask one child to travel to Scotland for a tour of a wool mill, then on to Ireland for a tour of a crystal factory, after which he'll take a train to Paris for a stop at the Louvre, and eventually wind up in Madrid for a bullfight. Afterward, the next player might hop from London to Paris, then on to Munich and Switzerland. Each player charts a route using his or her marker as each country or city is announced. In the end you've enjoyed a whirlwind "tour" together.

Celebrating Holidays All Year Long (and Learning in the Process)

I've already discussed the concept of learning geography from *national* holidays throughout the year; there are many other ways to explore places, people, and cultures through additional festivities. Families worldwide celebrate life through carnivals, fairs, religious and historical holidays, seasonal festivals, and rites of passage.

You've already seen ways to expand your family's understanding of geography by including games, recipes, and fun. The following activities will take your children farther, you'll enjoy more time together, and the true test of learning will be measured in memories that last a lifetime:

CHRISTIAN HOLIDAYS

265 Beginning with Christmas, rally the family together to make a nativity scene during Holy Week (the week before Christmas). Gather paper tubes, Styrofoam balls, and papier maché compound. Study various manger scenes, then produce a three-dimensional replica of a favorite. Paint the dried characters with tempera paints, and seal them with acrylic spray. Throughout the process, discuss how nativity scenes are used in various Christmas celebrations around the world.

266 Find a library book that explains Yule logs and the Swedish celebration of Christmas, then construct your own centerpiece together. Prepare the traditional hot spiced fruit soup for Christmas morning with dried apricots, apples, currants, cinnamon, and cider, and enjoy the beverage as the children begin opening their gifts.

267 Paint a family Christmas mural (on an oversized sheet of poster board or primed canvas) depicting celebrations from around the world. For example, you'll want to include a Christmas cactus, a crown of lights, a nativity scene, wooden shoes stuffed with candies, and so on. Ask your children to gather information and pictures to use as references. Keep in mind that a cooperative effort is more important than artistic skill; when your mural is done, each painter should sign the work.

268 Read about St. Nicholas (patron saint of children) and put on a play for family and friends. Dressed as a bishop, and wearing a white wig and beard (made from craft fur), your young child can imitate Sinterklaas riding a white horse (an adult with a white sheet over his back) through the streets of Amsterdam.

269 The Easter festival provides an opportunity to explore the tradition of Easter eggs, which are symbols of new life. Patterned eggs actually came from the Ukraine; your children can research traditional designs to replicate for your celebration. Instead of using hard-boiled eggs, try creating works of art with colorful polymer clays—or make jeweled eggs with self-hardening clay, beads, and paint.

270 An Easter banner is often used during liturgical services and in festival parades around the globe. Your family can make one to hang on a wall during the season with felt, burlap, ribbons, and a wooden dowel. Older children can assist in designing the pieces and cutting them out, while younger children can glue designs in place. Consider elements from Spain and Italy when drawing and assembling the patterns, and discuss Easter celebrations in those countries as you work. Young children will enjoy a mock parade when the project is finished.

Jewish Holidays

Rosh Hashanah signals the beginning of a new year. For ten days, there is a period of self-examination, culminating with Yom Kippur (day of atonement). Your family can make a "tapestry" of the Ten Commandments during this holiday by drawing or painting a symbol for each of the commandments on a piece of material (cotton, muslin, canvas, felt, etc.). Add one symbol each day until the tapestry is completed on Yom Kippur, then look up Israel in a children's atlas and encyclopedia. Locate Mt. Sinai together on a map.

272 Build a menorah at Hanukkah with any pliable wire. There are nine stems in a Hanukkah menorah; ask your children to find a picture of one. Plan the design with an older child. Keep it simple. You can bend the wire to form nine branches from a "trunk" of nine wires that have been twisted securely for strength. Shape the end of each branch into a candleholder and press the trunk into self-hardening clay or plaster (formed in the bottom of a clean margarine tub). During the eight nights of Hanukkah, read about Syria and the story of the holiday.

273 Make candles to fit your family's menorah. You can use rolled beeswax or dip long strands of twine into melted paraffin (younger children need adult assistance and supervision). Use white and blue wax to match the colors of Israel's flag and add gold star-shaped stickers when they've cooled.

274 Passover is a celebration of freedom and incorporates an appreciation for spring (when the earth is free of winter's chill). Gather everyone in the kitchen to make Haroset: place ½ cup of shelled walnuts, 3 apples (peeled, cored, and sliced), ¼ cup of grape juice, and 1 teaspoon of cinnamon in a blender or food processor. Gently purée the ingredients, then refrigerate for at least one day before serving. Using an atlas or map, help your children trace the path that Moses and the Israelites followed when they fled Egypt. What cities are near there today? What kind of terrain is in that area? Where did the Israelites finally settle? Explain that the soil was fertile in this promised land, which is why the Passover celebration includes sweet treats.

Family Holidays

275 Bake a cake together on January 6 in celebration of France's Family Day. A simple packaged cake mix is fine, but have your children stir a few candy "charms" into the batter before you pour it into pans. (When choosing your candy, avoid anything that may be a choking hazard for small children.) Bake, cool, and frost this treasure cake, and serve it after dinner, carefully searching each slice for hidden candy. The first child to find a candy charm gets to wear a crown. Make the golden crown simply and easily by cutting a piece of foil poster board and stapling it into a crown shape to fit a child's head.

276 Celebrate the Turkish holiday *Egemenlik Bayrami* (Children's Day) on April 23 with kite flying, a puppet show, and cake. To make puppets for a family show, have your children decorate muslin gardening gloves with felt-tipped markers. The fingers can either represent individual faces (a crowd of onlookers), a jester's funny hat, or locks of hair (with a face drawn on the palm). Encourage creativity. Look up Turkey in an atlas or encyclopedia and help your children make kites that resemble the country's flag. The kites can be diamond-shaped, rectangular, or shaped like a wind sock, and can be made from any material you have on hand (such as an old sheet, paper bags, etc.).

277 March 3 is *Hina-Matsuri* (Doll Festival) in Japan; celebrate by hosting a doll party for your daughter and her friends. Ask your daughter to help design special invitations. Bake her favorite cookies together. Decorate the table with a special cloth, fresh flowers, and tiny doll shoes at every place setting. If you have a traditional Japanese doll (or can find one), use it as a centerpiece. Encourage your daughter to explain the holiday to her guests, sharing her knowledge of the country in the process.

Various Seasonal Holidays

278 *Kwanza* takes place during the week between Christmas and New Year, and celebrates the harvest in Africa. Seven candles are placed in a candelabra: three red, three green, and one black (in the center). One candle is lit every night. Have your child check out a library book that explains the holiday, and expand your reading to include information about Africa. Enjoy a game of Mancala—an ancient game originally played with jewels—which is now available in toy stores for about $10.

279 A springtime celebration called *Holi* is certain to be a hit with children of all ages. The Hindu festival takes place in March or April (their calendar varies from ours), and children are encouraged to squirt each other with colored water. Before the fun begins, read about India and Nepal together. Your children might want to wrap old sheets—sari style—around their swimsuit-covered bodies before dousing each other outside. If you use tubes of children's washable watercolor paints, the color should wash out of your children's clothes. A little concentrated pigment goes a long way, so use only a few drops of color per squirt gun.

280 Budding sailors will want to celebrate the Chinese Dragon Boat festival in early June. Your children can build, carve, or purchase a toy boat for this event. Hold a boat party in your backyard "marina" for all of their friends, using a wading pool to test the sails of each boat. Read the story of *Ping* (a favorite children's book) to the group and serve Chinese finger foods.

Ask your children to help you find other holidays, celebrations, or interesting ways to learn about the world together.

CHAPTER

The Three Rs: Reasoning, Responsibility, and Respect

Ah, to have perfect little angels residing in our homes. It would be delightful, wouldn't it? We all experience those rare, magical moments when cooperation reigns—when our bright offspring take the initiative and demonstrate flawless consideration for others. However, children are children, and even a genius can get on your last raw nerve occasionally.

"It's Not Fair!" and Other Battle Cries

The following scene may sound familiar:

"I was watching cartoons!"

"Well, it's time for *my* show. You've already been watching TV for half an hour!"

"Mom! Jason changed the channel and I was watching something!"

"But it's my turn to watch! Tell her it's my turn to watch, Mom!"

Grabbing the remote control, you turn the television off and announce, "*Enough*. The TV is off until after dinner. Jason, did you do your homework?"

"It's not *fair!*" the little one cries, "I was watching cartoons!"

Your son crosses his arms and sulks. "I'll do my homework before bed."

"You'll do your homework *now*," you say, "and you'll put it in your daypack when you're done."

"It's not fair!" he moans. "I *never* get to do what I want to do!"

Children have very strong feelings about what is or isn't fair—and often their definition rests on whether they got what they wanted. As they mature, they'll learn to become flexible, imaginative, cooperative, open, responsible, decisive, and purposeful in their efforts to meet their needs and wants. Right now, though, they're just beginning to learn the consequences of actions (or inactions), and you can *show* them how to problem-solve. Consider the following "prime-time whines" and ideas for getting past them:

281 **"It's *mine*, and I don't have to share!"** When your preschooler refuses to share his toys, try demonstrating the flip side: when he asks you for a piece of your cake, a sip of your drink, something out of your purse, and so on, refuse him. Chances

are good he'll be shocked if you repeat the very words he uses. Give your message a moment to really sink in, then ask him how he feels. Explain that his little friends feel the same way when he refuses to share his toys. Ask him to think about how else he might answer a request to share; suggest that he take turns with his favorite toys during the next play date.

282 **"I'll do it later!"** When you've asked your child a dozen times to pick up her room or empty the trash, and she continues to ignore your requests, hold a mini-strike. For example, she probably expects you to wash and fold her clothes, right? What if you didn't do that for one week? When she comes to you and announces that she's out of clean underwear, tell her you'll do it later. Repeat the process every time she mentions her laundry. Eventually she'll get frustrated or confused, and at that time you have a perfect opportunity to point out that you feel the same way when she puts off her chores. Depending on your child, laundry might not work (adolescent boys, for example, aren't notoriously cleanly), but you get the idea.

283 **"I never get to do anything I want to do!"** When those whined words have worn away your patience, adopt a (verbal) child-like attitude toward your own responsibilities. Postpone making dinner; after work, simply change your clothes, sink into your favorite chair with a book, and wait. Inevitably someone will ask when dinner will be served. Be dramatic. Act as if you're under great duress, toss the book onto the floor, and whine, "I never get to do what I want!" Repeat the process with all of the household duties that your children normally see you do. When they look at you as if you're losing your mind,

point out that we all have responsibilities that occasionally interfere with what we'd really like to be doing.

284 **"I hate vegetables! Why do I have to eat vegetables?!"** Embark on a simple scientific experiment to demonstrate why balanced nutrition is important; purchase two small (identical) plants from a nursery or garden shop and place both in a sunny window. Water one of them when appropriate, but water the other one infrequently. Fertilize the more frequently watered plant, but don't fertilize the other. Within a month, even a very young child can recognize the difference between the plant that was fed and watered carefully and the one that was not. Explain that balanced meals—like fertilizer does for plants—help children grow, but that as people we have many different foods to choose from. Ask your children to list favorite vegetables or to find vegetable recipes they'd be willing to try; let them help you prepare the recipes.

285 **"I can't do it! It's too hard!"** This is a common complaint among children ages six to ten, who are sometimes overwhelmed and easily frustrated. Rather than jumping in to "help" your child, encourage his confidence. For example, if he's working on a special project and finds himself stuck, validate his feelings without telling him how to solve the dilemma: "I understand how frustrating that is, but I also know you're a smart boy. Where can you look this up?" Ask leading questions and he'll start to problem-solve. Afterward, praise his efforts and remind him that you knew he could do it all along. If he isn't happy with his results, ask more questions to help him see what he learned, then encourage him to try again.

286 **"She's so mean! I wish she'd never been born!"** When sibling fights erupt, try this: ask your angry child to describe a day without her sister or brother. The first musings will be enthusiastic. Next, if you know which activities she enjoys with her sibling, ask her about those: "Who would you play Barbies with?" or "Who'd be the student when you play school?" Your child may list the names of friends; if she does, ask her, "What if Kelsey moved away?" or "What if Erin made a new friend and didn't want to come over to play with you as often?" When your child thinks about the answers to those questions, point out that even though a brother or sister can be frustrating at times, there are benefits to having a sibling, too.

287 **"It's not fair! Everyone else's parents let them __________."** This statement calls for a game of "if/then." Start the word game with simple statements, asking your child to fill in the blanks. For example: "If we sit down for a meal at noon, then we're eating __________." or "If I step into a deep puddle, then my feet will get __________." Ask your child several questions and have him develop some of his own. As you continue the game, move into problem areas, such as: "If you didn't do your homework, then your teacher would __________." or "If I didn't get enough sleep, then I'd be __________ the next day." Gradually expand the game to include what might happen next. "If I didn't get enough sleep, then I'd be tired the next day and I might __________." Next, focus on the issue at hand. Let's say your child wants to stay up later and watch questionable television shows. You disapprove. Your next game statement might be: "If you went to bed at 10:00, then you'd get less sleep and you might be tired the next day. If you were tired, then you might __________." The game helps your child discover the reason behind your refusal. Through

your dialogue, you might also be able to work out a compromise if one is appropriate.

Try not to expect an immediate end to all family strife. In my late thirties, I still feel like whining, complaining, or rebelling at times; don't you? When it seems that there are more things on my "to do" list than there are hours in the day, I'd like to revert to childish behavior. Parents and children alike have bad days. When we come together as a team, though, we tend to have more good days and fewer bad ones. Simply speaking, no one person can do it all.

Raising a Thinking Child is a resource for parents and teachers who want to help children master conflict resolution. Through a program called ICPS (I Can Problem Solve), Dr. Myrna B. Shure's techniques are widely used by elementary school guidance counselors. The principles of ICPS are based on open, effective communication between child and adult. Special dialogues, activities, and games are listed in the book.

What Children Learn When They Take Out the Trash

The mere thought of "doing chores" can bring a silent groan to adults and children alike because—let's be honest—scooping out the cat box isn't anyone's idea of fun. In fact, all of us could rattle off lists of unpleasant duties, but we know that chores don't cease to exist because they're ignored.

Do you remember the movie *Mary Poppins?* Mary Poppins and her two little charges had a lot of fun while tidying up the nursery; they made a game of it. Okay, Mary Poppins was a magical nanny—and I don't expect families across the country to start singing and dancing while wiping the bathroom floor—but a combined effort can make the job easier. In the process of working together, you'll be teaching your children:

- Responsibility
- Determination
- The rewards of a solid work ethic
- The importance of a positive attitude
- Consistency between words and actions
- Generosity
- Self-discipline
- Consideration for others

- The importance of community and teamwork

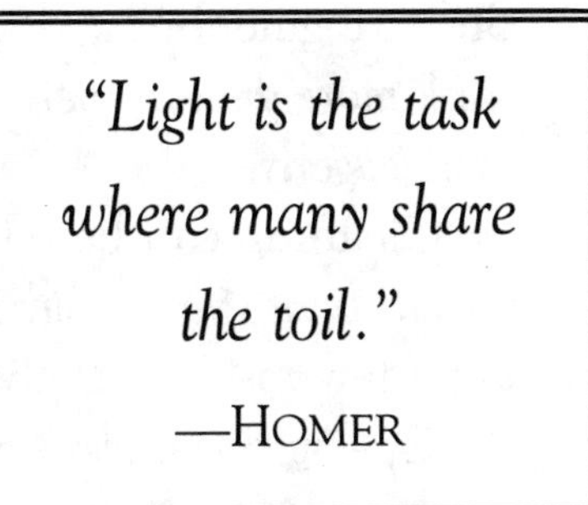

> *"Light is the task where many share the toil."*
>
> —HOMER

All in all, that's an impressive list of lessons from something as simple as taking out the trash—but there's more! As a busy parent, *you also benefit from involving your children in the day-to-day household routines*. Sure, it might be faster and easier to do the housework yourself, but if you involve your children you'll reap:

- More time (as their skills and abilities develop)

- Less pressure or stress

- A clearer understanding of each child's temperament, strengths, and weaknesses
- Closer relationships within the family circle
- Their appreciation for all that you do on their behalf

Motivate your helpers with a reward: allowance is a time-honored motivator, but you could also plan a special activity at the end of the week to celebrate a job well done. If you're like me, it might be a good idea to lower your standards a bit. I'd love a home that looks like it jumped from the pages of a magazine, but if the drawers and closets aren't coordinated and organized according to Martha Stewart guidelines, does it really matter? *Reward a willingness to work more than the perfection of the task and your children will pitch in more eagerly.*

Cleaning can be educational as well. *When they do chores on a regular basis, your children can improve their grades.* How? Well, here are a few tasks your children can do—listed according to age and ability—and the lessons they'll learn from them:

Preschool Children

Pick up toys when they're through playing [sorting, organization, spatial concepts]

Empty small wastebaskets [gravity]

Sort dirty laundry into piles of whites, lights, and darks [color identification, sorting]

Dust furniture [particles/matter, gravity]

Straighten books, magazines, pillows, etc. [spatial concepts, symmetry]

Mop up small spills [depending on the spill, primitive physics or chemistry]

Fold clothes [organization, sorting, symmetry]

Collect trash from sidewalk or yard [sorting, gravity, basic ecology]

Pull weeds in flower beds [plant identification, sorting, ecology]

Assist with cooking [basic chemistry and physics, organization, concept of time]

Set the dinner table [spatial concepts, organization, object relationships]

Kindergarten Through Third Grade

299 Keep bedroom clean, including making the bed, putting away clothes, etc. [organization, self-discipline, creativity, symmetry, esthetics]

Put away folded laundry [sorting, organization, problem solving]

Clean sinks and mirrors in bathroom [chemistry, self-discipline, problem solving]

Load unbreakable dishes and blunt utensils into dishwasher [sorting, spatial relationships, organization, some chemistry and ecology]

Help put away the groceries [sorting, organization, physics, flexibility]

Planting flowers, raking leaves, and other simple yard chores [botany, ecology, sorting, self-discipline, problem solving, flexibility]

Assist with meal planning and preparation [chemistry, physics, organization, creativity, problem solving, cooperation]

Make own lunch [organization, creativity, nutrition, problem solving, flexibility]

Feed pets [zoology, nutrition, empathy, self-discipline]

Fourth Grade Through Middle School

Assist with meal planning and grocery shopping [nutrition, organization, time management, flexibility, mathematics/budgeting]

Help prepare family meals [time management, chemistry, physics, problem solving, nutrition]

Load and unload dishwasher [spatial relationships, sorting, organization, problem solving, chemistry]

Help wash, dry, and fold laundry [spatial relationships, chemistry, physics, ecology, symmetry]

Care for younger siblings [interpersonal effectiveness, management, cooperation, empathy]

Clean the basement or garage [sorting, flexibility, problem solving, organization, ecology]

Mow the lawn [botany, ecology, physics, self-discipline, flexibility, endurance]

Take out the trash [spatial relationships, ecology, problem solving, self-discipline]

Vacuum and/or mop floors [particles/matter, gravity, self-discipline, problem solving, endurance]

Distribute incoming mail [sorting, organization]

Depending on your family or lifestyle, there may be other chores that can be assigned to your children. By thinking about what's involved with each task, you'll uncover a multitude of educational opportunities as you establish your "home team."

Role-Playing Games, Role-Reversal Games, and Family Unity

Have you ever been to a college or minor-league baseball game? If the catcher doesn't understand the pitcher's job, it's unlikely that the team will win a tournament; if the pitcher doesn't know where the second baseman is, the opposing team will score. Each player has a designated role; in order to play effectively, the team members must understand every position.

Do your children understand your position? Do you understand each of theirs? Unlike a baseball team, some family roles fluctuate regularly. For example, in single-parent homes children sometimes alternate between parents weekly, monthly, or semiannually. Even in traditional families (where both parents are present), long hours at the office can upset the balance of roles within the family dynamic. And our children grow; yesterday's toddler suddenly sprouts a whisker or two on his chin, or your little ballerina takes an after-school baby-sitting job. We have to work at getting and staying connected.

Here are a few fun games designed to keep you playing together and headed for the big leagues as you field the curve balls life throws your way:

Warming Up

318 Preschool-age children illustrate their concept of family through play. If you own a dollhouse, spend some time with your children simply playing; watch carefully to see if you can decipher their concepts of family roles. If you don't own a dollhouse, play "dress up" together—which works as well with small boys as it does young girls—and allow your children to make up an adult day. You'll get plenty of insights from a half hour of fun.

319 Collaborate with your young child and invent stories based on fictional families or fairy tales. Pattern the "family" after your own. Prompt your child's participation by asking questions such as: "What kind of home do they live in? What does it look like? How many children live there? What are their names?

Tell me about ______. Is she a nice sister?" Your child may trail off into discussing various memories or adventures, and that's okay. For example, he may describe a parent not as a doctor (which is the actual profession) but as a gardener, because his most vivid impressions of the parent revolve around gardening and flowers. Or he may describe a sibling as being away from the home, because his perception of that sibling hinges on long periods of separation during school hours. This is an activity that can easily blend with a family meal, and everyone can participate.

320 Another talking and "make believe" game encourages problem-solving skills while providing you with valuable clues to your child's needs. Think about a scenario that your child can identify with on some level, in which the main character faces a challenge or dilemma. For example: "Tara is a very creative girl who loves to draw and write. She dreams of someday writing children's books and becoming famous. Tara's teacher has asked her to work on the school paper, and her art teacher suggested that she also draw a comic strip for the paper. But now, every time Tara sits down to work, she gets nervous and stops because she thinks what she's writing is dumb and feels her cartoons aren't funny. What would you tell Tara if you were her friend?" Listen carefully to each child's response, because their advice tells you the kind of support each one needs when facing a problem.

Infield Practice

321 The Feelings game can either be conversational or written, depending on the ages of your children. Its purpose is to help your children recognize and identify their emotions, and at the same time offer you insights into their unique perspectives. The first step is to name various emotions, then ask each child to describe a moment or event that illustrates the feeling. For example, happiness might be described as "feeling good," and your children would talk about something that made them feel happy. Next, ask each child to guess what makes *you* happy. Continue this game using fear, anger, guilt, jealousy, embarrassment, confidence, and love (use positive emotions in the beginning and again at the end of the game).

322 The Who's Who in the Family? game makes for hilarious dinnertime banter. Taking turns, each person silently chooses a family member and offers word/phrase clues to the other players (who will try to guess the identity from the clues). For example, a brother who is older and larger, enjoys sports, reads comic books, and loves pizza might translate into top dog, big feet, shooting sphere, silly pictures, and tomato pie. After the first round of fun, start to incorporate personality traits into the clues. Next, add household responsibilities to the clues. You might try playing this game during a holiday gathering for easy entertainment.

323 Oh My Stars! is a similar game. Assign a secretary, then ask each player to think of someone whom he or she admires (this can be a famous person or a family member or friend) and a few special qualities that person possesses. Each player takes turns providing "personal quality" clues, which the other players use to guess the "star." The secretary records the names of the "stars" as they're correctly guessed. After all the stars have been guessed, the secretary reads each name again from her "star list." As each name is read, the players list as many "star qualities" as they can remember hearing about each name. Finally, the secretary reads the list of "star qualities," and the players try to match those qualities to qualities held by family members. This game will help build virtue, self-esteem, and appreciation for others.

Outfield Practice

324 Play a negative/positive role-reversal game with your children. Taking turns, each family member pretends to be the mother, father, sister, or brother doing or saying something negative, and then "correcting" the behavior by demonstrating a positive alternative. For example, a child might pretend to be a parent hollering about a messy bedroom. Then that same child (again pretending to be a parent) could offer a reward for cleaning the bedroom, close the bedroom door, or some other alternative to shouting. A parent reversing roles with a child might throw a tantrum because she didn't win a board game, then demonstrate how she could congratulate the winner in spite of her disappointment. Guard against hurt feelings by keeping exaggeration to a minimum, and encourage plenty of discussion.

325 Follow up the negative/positive role-reversal game with a story game called My Misunderstood Monster. Each family member, having witnessed his or her own negative behaviors, creates a monster character to explain what might be behind that behavior. For example: The Yodeling Yellow Yox doesn't think anyone can hear him, so he yodels and yells in order to be heard. Or Teerexia Antrum feels frustrated but doesn't know what to do, so she throws herself in the floor and cries. Younger children might need help from an older sibling or parent to develop their character; encourage imagination. By defining the emotions behind the behavior, everyone will have a better understanding of their own reactions—and the reactions of others in the family.

326 Designing bumper stickers can help family members work through negative attitudes quickly and easily;

before you know it, everyone will be laughing. Gather several pieces of paper and pass them out with pencils, pens, or markers. Ask everyone to get in a really rotten mood. Tell them you're opening a bumper sticker factory, and their job is to think up negative or rebellious sayings, such as: "I don't want a hug, I want a dirt bike!" or "I may be small, but I'm loud!" Afterward, talk about how you'll market your bumper stickers. Ask your children who might buy them and why. Their answers might uncover new ways to deal with conflicts, because you'll understand where the negative attitude is coming from.

327 To help each other work through mild or major irritations, try a game called Bug Zapper. Every family member tells the others about a pet peeve. The listeners offer suggestions to zap what bugs you. For example: as a busy mother, long lines at the bank or grocery store really bug me. My fellow players might offer suggestions to help distract me if I'm caught in a long line. Next, players take turns assuming roles. In my case, one of my children might pretend to be me waiting at the checkstand of a busy grocery store. He could demonstrate what I'd look like bugged, and then waiting patiently. Every family member gets a turn to present a bug and to zap others; everyone should join in the act.

Batter Up!

328 Let your children demonstrate their understanding of service by planning an evening at KidServe Restaurant. Decide on a menu together (one that your children can easily prepare). The children will draw menus, set the table, and prepare a simple meal. They will act as hosts, waiters, busboys, and so on

throughout dinner. Encourage lots of fun with this game; it's a great way to build self-esteem, cooperation, participation, and sensitivity. You'll want to reward their efforts with a generous tip!

329 What are your children's dreams? Do they know yours? They will when you play Dream Weavers together! Each player is asked to think about his or her daydreams. Taking turns, players describe a favorite daydream. To make this more interesting (and to spark deeper thought), ask your children such questions as: "If this daydream were real, what kinds of things would you have done to make it happen?" or "How would you feel if this daydream were real?" Be sure to share your own daydreams (G-rated ones, of course!).

330 How does your family spell "relief"? Ask your children to name as many people, places, things, or activities as they can that bring them comfort. Write their responses on a sheet of paper and share some of your own. Next, develop a short story together, using some of the words of comfort from your list. For example: "Once upon a time, there was a small creature named Zig who had a very bad day. Zig decided to take a *walk* to his *grandmother's* house and hoped she would give him a cup of *hot chocolate* . . ." Involve your children as the story develops and let them get silly. Who knows? This could eventually become an activity that spells "relief" for them.

331 Start an Appreciation Collection. At the end of each day, ask your children to think of one thing that happened that made them feel good inside. Write each thing on a small slip of paper. Deposit these slips in an empty coffee can. Encourage your children to include appreciation for each other, such as:

"Jennifer helped me pick up the toys. That was nice and I felt good." At the end of each month, pull out all the slips of paper after dinner one night and read them aloud as a family. This way, you have a regular reminder of all that is good in your life, and your children can see the benefits of kindness.

HOME RUN

332 Conduct a family survey, asking each member to complete the following statements: My greatest strength is __________. My parents' greatest strengths are __________ and __________. My brother's (or sister's) greatest strength is __________. My greatest achievement is __________. My parents' greatest achievements are __________ and __________. My brother's (or sister's) greatest achievement is __________. Based on my strengths and achievements, in the next ten years I could __________. Based on their strengths and achievements, my family members could help me by __________, and I could help them __________. When everyone is finished, discuss what you learned about each other.

333 Enlist the help of your children and write an advertisement about your family. Pretend that you're going to place the ad in your local newspaper to let your community know about your family's lifestyle, activities, strengths, and combined gifts. Scour your newspaper's business section for company advertisements to use as templates for your own ad. You'll need to develop a slogan and a mission statement, such as: "The Griffith family lives to learn and learns to give," followed by: "We believe that little minds are interested in the extraordinary and that education—combined with imagination—leads to extraordinary service." Once you have your slogan or mission statement

written, think about ways to describe your "company" and its employees.

Volunteering Together to Make a Greater Impact

Did you belong to a scouting organization when you were a child? If you did, then perhaps you remember singing carols to the residents of a nursing home during the Christmas season or picking up litter at a park. Maybe your troop raked leaves, collected canned goods, or held a car wash to raise money for a local charity.

Children are natural philanthropists; even a two-year-old will offer a cherished toy to a crying playmate. Children want to make a difference, to reach out to others—to give. Charitable acts bolster empathy, self-esteem, and values while laying the foundation for strong moral character. We all want to raise thinking children, but we also want to produce young adults who demonstrate kindness, caring, integrity, and leadership.

> *"A good heart is better than all the heads in the world."*
> —EDWARD BULWER-LYTTON

Our children watch us constantly (isn't that a frightening thought?) and their most powerful education comes not from textbooks but from our example. When we're involved with charities or nonprofit organizations, we demonstrate the power and rewards of giving. Maybe you already participate in volunteer activities or give to a worthwhile charity or two. If so, you're to be applauded! You're providing your children with the gift of heart, and the world will be a better place because of it. If you're not, don't feel guilty.

Trust me, I understand the full meaning of the word *busy*. With two young boys, an upwardly mobile husband, two home-based businesses, home education, several hobbies, and a household to run—not to mention a number of other activities that get squeezed into my schedule—sleep deprivation is a common phenomenon for this busy Mom. How can I find time in an already overbooked day to get involved? How can you?

We can all make a difference in simple ways by investing a little bit of time or money as a family. Involve your children as you research potential charities or community projects. Children will reap priceless rewards from hardly more than five minutes once a month—more if you can spare it.

Fast and Easy Financial Support (a.k.a. Writing a Check and Sealing an Envelope)

- Audubon Society: 700 Broadway, New York, NY 10003
- Better Boys Foundation: 1512 S. Pulaski, Chicago, IL 60623
- Big Brothers/Big Sisters of America: 230 N. 13th Street, Philadelphia, PA 19107
- Boys and Girls Clubs of America: 1230 W. Peachtree Street NW, Atlanta, GA 30309
- Catholic Charities: 1731 King Street, Suite 200, Alexandria, VA 22314
- Child Welfare League of America: 440 First Street NW, Third Floor, Washington, DC 20001
- Children's Defense Fund: 25 E Street NW, Washington, DC 20001

- Christian Children's Fund: 2821 Emerywood Parkway, Richmond, VA 23261
- Global Action: 740 Front Street, Santa Cruz, CA 95060
- Kids For Kids, Inc.: 469 W. 57th Street, New York, NY 10019

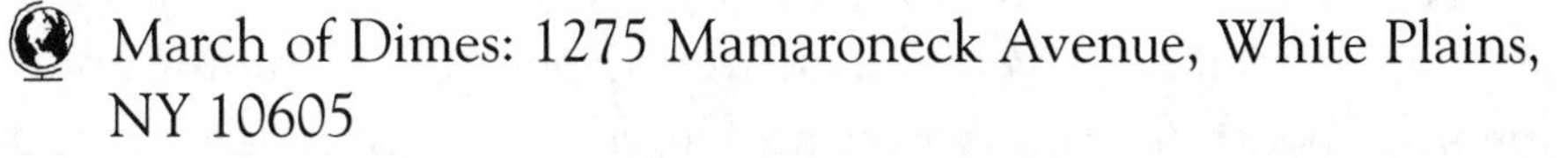

- March of Dimes: 1275 Mamaroneck Avenue, White Plains, NY 10605
- National Committee to Prevent Child Abuse: 332 S. Michigan Avenue, Suite 1600, Chicago, IL 60604
- National Wildlife Federation: 1400 Sixteenth Street NW, Washington, DC 20036
- Sierra Club: 730 Polk Street, San Francisco, CA 94109
- UNICEF: call 1-800-FOR-KIDS to ask for information and a copy of *Kids Helping Kids* magazine

ONE-DAY-PER-MONTH, PUSH-UP-YOUR-SLEEVES CHARITIES (A.K.A. ESCAPING THE PHONE AND FAX)

334 Build a better future for an underprivileged family, one nail at a time, by contacting Habitat for Humanity at 1-800-422-4828 for a project near you.

335 Cook or serve up hope and understanding by volunteering to help with meals once a month at a homeless shelter. Call 1-800-88-SHELTER for more information about volunteer opportunities in your city.

336 Volunteer to cook or deliver a meal to an ailing or elderly neighbor. Several organizations can help you locate someone in need if you don't already have a neighbor in mind. Contact Meals on Wheels, Social Services, or your hospital's elderly care coordinator for more information about their programs.

337 Demonstrate your family's heart for good health by stuffing envelopes, answering phones, or staffing an information booth for the American Heart Association. Call 1-800-242-8721 to get in contact with a local coordinator.

338 Celebrate survival by volunteering with the American Cancer Society. Every year, local chapters host a "Cancer Survivors Day," complete with food, fanfare, and fun. Your children will enjoy dishing up smiles—and they'll learn about the strength and tenacity that helps us all overcome illness or adversity. Contact your local chapter by looking under American Cancer Society in your telephone book.

339 Friendship comes in all ages and stages when your family visits a local nursing home on a regular basis. Check your local Yellow Pages under "Nursing Care" or "Senior Care" for the address and phone number of a nursing home near your house. Ask about adopt-a-grandparent programs.

340 Do you know of someone who could use a little help around the house? In one afternoon, you can mow a lawn, clean rain gutters, tidy up a home, or run errands; in a weekend, your family can paint a small house, repair an appliance, or patch a leaky roof.

341 Get involved with the American Red Cross and let your children hand out orange juice and cookies after a blood drive. Look in your local Yellow Pages for a Red Cross chapter near you.

342 Help spread the word that drinking and driving don't mix and give your children the strength to stand up to peer pressure. Contact your local Mothers Against Drunk Driving (MADD) and find out how you can get involved in local programs.

343 Literacy is the key to success, and your family can underwrite success stories throughout your town or city by contacting Reading Is Fundamental (202-287-3257) for information about family literacy programs in your area. Your children will love to show off their reading skills as they inspire other children through shared books, activities, and fun.

344 If you own a home-based business, use it as the foundation for a fund-raising campaign in support of local schools or organizations. Many companies (including Avon, Discovery Toys, Mary Kay, and Tupperware) provide fund-raising information for their representatives. But you can also base a campaign on any kind of business: if you have a secretarial service, you can ask clients to donate extra money; if you have a housekeeping business, you can organize a clean-a-thon. Involve your children, and they'll learn that success is more than an income level.

345 Make a difference in your community; fight hunger and poverty with the help of Share Our Strength. Call 1-800-969-4767 for volunteer opportunities in your area.

There are dozens of ways to experience the power of giving as a family. Churches, synagogues, public schools, YMCAs, YWCAs, and parks and recreation departments always need help—financially and practically. Choose projects together and encourage your child's involvement. Rediscover idealism!

CHAPTER

Making the Grade

When you were in grade school, did you ever silently admire a bright red A+ at the top of your test paper? How did that grade make you feel? Smart? Successful? Maybe even a little smug? Did your parents celebrate your good grades?

Report cards are designed to measure a child's knowledge and comprehension of textbook material. Higher marks signify greater mastery, while lower grades sound a warning. Report cards serve a purpose in the education of a child, yet letter grades often hold more significance for adults than for the children to whom they're assigned. A teacher who's doling out mediocre marks to half a classroom of students can't help but realize that she's also scored a C. A father or mother fretting over a bad report card is almost certainly concerned about the school's impression of his or her effectiveness as a parent. In other words, report cards aren't just a measure of the child's proficiency; they also rate the successfulness of adult role models.

The Pros and Cons of Report Cards

What does a high grade-point average really mean? It means that the teacher has been successful in communicating the text material, the parents have instilled value and discipline at home, and the child has absorbed all required information. Straight As can also indicate intelligence—even genius. However, lower grades don't always point to a lack thereof.

Several of the greatest minds in history did poorly in school. Albert Einstein flunked the first grade. How could that be? Didn't his teacher recognize that this was *the* Albert Einstein—that his intelligence quotient went off the charts? Einstein wasn't alone. Thomas Edison was considered "disruptive" and received failing grades in school as well. That's the trouble with report cards; your child's genius may be overlooked because:

- She doesn't find the material interesting enough to explore
- She has difficulty sitting still for extended periods of time
- Her imagination overpowers the teacher's voice
- Her physical development temporarily takes precedence over cognitive development
- She possesses a different internal schedule, becoming "fresh" later in the day
- A family crisis or upheaval has prompted normal regression

- She's dealing with undiagnosed challenges (such as ADD, dyslexia, etc.)

As parents, we're eager to celebrate good report cards because, in our society, good grades are the pathway to a successful life. The important thing to remember is that a report card is the measurement of whether our children absorbed textbook material—not whether they're intelligent. In fact, most teachers, guidance counselors, and pediatricians agree that *curiosity* is a better measure of "genius" than grades are.

Think about the following questions. Does your child:

- Have an advanced vocabulary?
- Have an outstanding memory?
- Ask endless questions?
- Have many interests, hobbies, or collections?
- Have a passionate interest in a particular subject?
- Get totally absorbed in activity or thought?
- Show strong motivation for things that interest him, but appear unwilling to work on other activities?
- Show a reluctance to move from one subject area to another?
- Demonstrate abstract thinking?
- Prefer challenging tasks to easy ones?
- Have the ability to do two things at once (such as watching a ball game while doing homework)?
- Catch on quickly but resist doing the work?
- Resist direction, preferring her own methods?

- Show sensitivity toward others?
- Have a strong sense of fairness?
- Show an interest in global issues?
- Have a sophisticated sense of humor?
- See connections between apparently unconnected ideas or subjects?
- Prefer the company of adults?
- Prefer to work alone?
- Become bossy with other children?
- Talk incessantly?
- Exhibit "street smarts"?
- Display original ideas or elaborate on existing ideas?
- Use objects for something other than what they were intended for?
- Say what he thinks without regard for consequences?
- Seem absentminded about details?
- Love to play with words and ideas?
- Show a talent for fine arts?
- Experiment with ideas or hunches?
- Daydream frequently?
- Pursue nonconformity in dress, thought, or behavior?
- Receive praise for exceptional ability?
- Cry easily when frustrated?

- Work very slowly, in the hope of perfecting a task?
- Ask for a lot of help and/or reassurance?
- Deal poorly with criticism?
- Expect other people to be "perfect"?
- Resist challenging work for fear that his struggle will be obvious?
- Procrastinate so much that tasks are rarely completed?

If you answered "yes" to any of those questions, congratulations! According to the Dublin School District in central Ohio, your child is "gifted"! My point echoes the title of this book: *every* child is a genius in one way or another regardless of report-card grades.

Why Your Child Needs a Cheerleader and a Coach

If you could somehow attach a hidden camera to your child's clothing—recording every event during the day—you might be startled to discover just how much children have changed over the past few decades. The world they live in has changed as well.

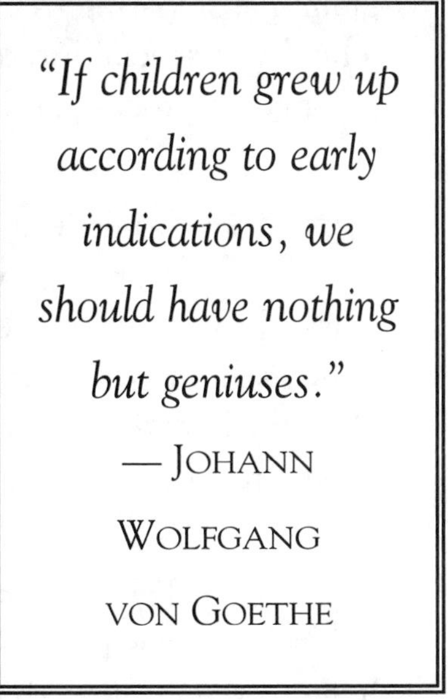

Progress is never all bad; in the areas of technology, social conscience, career possibilities, and available information the changes have mostly been for the good. There is, however, a price we've paid: family life is quickly being transformed; we're witnessing the birth of a "global village," rather than tightly knit local communities; and, in many ways, the period called childhood is shrinking. Our children process more information, have a greater number of choices, grapple with issues we'd never have imagined, and carry a higher level of stress than we did as children.

Does that sound bleak? It isn't. Parents today have an extraordinary advantage over parents of previous generations; we can utilize unbelievable amounts of tools and information to create a solid, nurturing, supportive, educational environment for ourselves and our children. Whether they attend public or private schools or are schooled at home, we can give our children the wings to soar beyond all expectations.

Get involved with your children, cheer them on, and coach them through rough spots with the following suggestions:

346 Demonstrate your commitment to education by taking a course at a junior college or university satellite program, participating in an online class, or attending a workshop on a hobby or special interest. Your children will see that education is an ongoing process, and that you're never too old to learn and grow.

347 Don't wait for parent-teacher conferences; introduce yourself to your child's teacher and stay in contact regularly throughout the year. If you have specific concerns about your child's school experience, discuss them in an open and friendly way. Do your best to recruit your child's teacher as a member of your "home team."

348 Try to volunteer time at your child's school—or in her classroom—at least once every semester. You don't have to spend more than half an hour overseeing a reading group or helping students with a special project, yet when you make that tiny investment you'll be giving your child the message that you really *care* about her education.

349 As much as possible, try to establish a predictable daily routine. Most children require consistency in order to feel secure; when they know what's expected of them and when, they're more likely to follow through with chores, homework, and other responsibilities.

350 Speaking of a schedule, your child needs time to tell you about his day. Pencil in at least five minutes every weekday afternoon or evening. If you're still at work when he gets home, arrange a predictable phone call. As much as you can, try not to rush him as he's talking. Give him your full attention and listen.

351 Try to anticipate your young child's needs. Does she have all the necessary supplies to do an assignment? Does she have enough time to accomplish her objective? Will she work better alone or in the company of others? How long has it been since she's eaten? She may need a snack before she tackles her homework. If there's an important function at her school, when should she arrive? What should she bring along?

352 Encourage your child's interests; help him balance the pursuit of those interests with established responsibilities. You might ask him to devise a plan that either incorporates his passions and duties or provides adequate time to accomplish necessary tasks *and* enjoy other activities.

353 Get to know the parents of some of your child's classmates. Introduce yourself at school functions, chat briefly in the hallway, or plan a small gathering during the holidays. This way, you'll know something about the homes your child might be playing in.

354 Celebrate successes *and* failures; buried inside every failure is a lesson that will lead to future success. Let your child know that the most important aspect of learning is the effort she puts into it—not the resulting grades.

> *"I have gotten a lot of results. I know several thousand things that won't work."*
>
> —THOMAS EDISON

355 Though this might seem contradictory, don't try to rescue your child from a problem or struggle. If you jump in to fix things for him, he might start to see himself as incapable of taking on a challenge; he may even stop thinking for himself. Instead, encourage his developing problem-solving skills.

356 Ease into uncharted waters together. If your child is changing schools, beginning homeschooling, facing a medical problem, entering puberty, or facing a similar challenge, allow for a period of transition and then work together to redefine goals, expectations, and relationships both inside and outside of the family.

Encourage learning but don't demand it—even if you're homeschooling. Become your child's cheerleader, information provider, and resource as you guide her natural development. Think about it this way: from the time she starts walking and talking, your child's instinctive inclination is to establish an identity apart from her parents; rebellion is a natural and expected part of growing up. If you're her "teacher," and she's rebelling against *you*, she may also rebel against learning in general.

358 Work with (rather than against) your child's temperament. Our oldest son, for example, was born with the intensity of a 1400-watt bulb. He's always been easy to entertain and has always pursued many and varied interests. However, he's a perfectionist with a low threshold for frustration. I could no more expect him to "relax" and "not worry" about an unsolved problem than I could squeeze my thighs into size-six jeans. It isn't going to happen. Insisting that he change his basic personality would merely escalate his frustration.

359 Along the same lines, understand that you can only do what you can do; the rest is up to your child. Don't accept responsibility for every problem your child faces during his school years. The truth is that sometimes you *can* help, but sometimes you *can't*.

360 Sincerely believe that your child can overcome any hurdle. If you don't believe she can do it, neither will she.

361 No matter what, give your child plenty of love; no child is "too old" or "too big" to hug (even one with newly sprouted whiskers).

362 Take care of yourself! When your children know that you're okay—that you're reasonably happy, productive, and valuable—it gives them the freedom to test their own wings without fear or worry. They know that someone strong and capable loves them enough to catch them if they fall.

PTAs, PTOs, and Other Support Systems Available to Parents

I remember a time, during a particularly stressful period in our lives, when I would gladly have paid any price to have my Mom and Pop under our roof, comforting, nurturing, and taking over where I felt incompetent. Let me put it another way: I've occasionally defined a "good day" as one in which I've managed to get dressed, feed my sons, and *not* flood the kitchen. I think we all have days (or weeks, or months) like that.

Where can you go when you need empathy, understanding, and support? If you're lucky, you have extended family that lives nearer than three thousand miles away—and you have good relationships with them. If not, at least you're in good company!

Parent/Teacher Associations (PTAs) and Organizations (PTOs) were designed to help build bridges between home and school; these are the obvious people to turn to when you're dealing with school-related concerns. Unfortunately, they're a resource that's barely tapped. Busy parents today have very little time to spare for involvement in such programs. Have you been to a PTA meeting lately? Attendance could probably stand a little boost. Make it a point to show up for at least one meeting per semester—if for no other reason than to meet a few allies.

What if you truly *can't* attend any PTA meetings, are home-schooling, or find yourself in an area without such a resource? In the Resources section at the back of this book, you will find a list of books, organizations, and other helpful sources to which you can refer.

Also, don't forget about local churches, synagogues, cooperatives, special-interest groups, counseling services, and Internet Service Providers (ISPs), such as America Online or CompuServe—both of which offer resources and support for parents and families.

Does My Child Need a Tutor?

Every parent occasionally discovers that a child's problem doesn't seem to be improving as quickly or easily as was hoped. It's also not uncommon for a teacher to exert a bit of pressure when the child's problem is perceived as disruptive to the flow of classroom activity. The bottom line is that sometimes—no matter what we've tried—our children hit a wall with learning. It might be a normal developmental phase or it might indicate a more serious situation. How can we tell the difference? When should we call a tutor?

First of all, you know your child better than anyone else does. Try to determine whether the problem stems from the text material, the general educational approach, an overcrowded classroom, a harried lifestyle, or difficulty understanding basic concepts. For example:

- Review your child's textbooks. If they're either boring or confusing to you, chances are good that she feels the same way about them. In this case, meet with the teacher or the principal (or both) and request alternative material. If the school denies your request, bring some fun and interesting books, games, or supplemental materials into your own home.

- The educational approach used in your child's classroom may not mesh with his basic temperament, learning style, or personality. In Chapter 10, you'll be able to identify his learning style. Try to incorporate activities that help him learn; he may need additional books, tapes, videos, toys, or games to help him grasp the material.
- Visit your child's classroom. How would you rate the noise level? The rowdiness level? Does the teacher seem to have control over the students? Is the teacher able to give adequate attention to the children who need it? Watch your child interact with her classmates. Does she seem anxious? Withdrawn? If you feel the classroom environment is at the foundation of your child's problem, ask the school to assign her to another teacher.
- Consider your child's daily schedule. If the family calendar is filled with several days' worth of after-school activities each week—and especially if your child appears tired and listless or lacks interest in formerly passionate pursuits—*simplify* before you enlist a tutor. Decide which activities can be dropped, scale your office hours back to a reasonable level, and spend a little more time enjoying each other.
- When the textbooks don't appear to be unusually dull, the educational approach works with your child's learning style, the classroom is well managed, and your child has plenty of free time yet his problems persist, involve your pediatrician. He can rule out illness, allergy, and vision or hearing problems and can help pinpoint whether you're dealing with a learning disability. Ask your pediatrician to interact with the school—possibly enlisting the school psychologist's input—in order to establish a reliable diagnosis and plan of action.

If long hours at work or outside commitments prevent you from tutoring your child yourself, this would be the time to set up an appointment with a paid ally. Ask friends or neighbors for referrals, contact the school district's administration office for a list of retired or substitute teachers, or call a local university for the names of students who tutor children.

CHAPTER

Keeping It All in Perspective

Your first child is an experiment; you bring your tiny, wriggling baby into a home brimming with books and magazines designed to help you raise this helpless being. Every volume and every glossy page was written so that new parents can know what to expect and when to expect it. Like you, I brought our firstborn home with great expectations and a few insecurities—and, like you, I soon discovered that many of the "experts" in baby and child development disagree about a lot of things.

One book told me to have as much body-to-body contact with my infant as possible every day, to bring him either into our bed or next to it, and to never let him "cry it out." Another book explained that I needed to provide our baby with plenty of colorful stimulation, get him used to a bed (and room) of his own, and delay gratification upon occasion. I was very confused. I couldn't think of a way to strap a baby and toys to my body, sleep in his crib with him, or delay gratification without listening to him howl. First-time parents quickly learn that there is no such thing as a by-the-book baby; neither of my sons did anything exactly according to published schedules. I eventually learned to trust myself and my children.

> *"Perhaps the greatest social service that can be rendered by anybody to the country and to mankind is to bring up a family."*
> —George Bernard Shaw

Understanding the Stages of Childhood

The bottom line is that there are *some* generalities that apply to *most* children, but each child develops according to his or her own internal clock, temperament, basic personality, and level of interest. A baby who starts out very alert and responsive to stimulation might nevertheless sit, crawl, or walk later than her peers. A toddler who can recite the Pledge of Allegiance before he's potty-trained may still struggle with early attempts at reading. If your child isn't developing according to published timelines, don't worry.

To parents, it sometimes feels like a particular stage is never going to end. I remember wondering more than once if I'd wind up with a son in diapers as he left for college, or if he'd still be hurling himself to the floor and screaming while carrying a briefcase. I was reasonably certain that I'd always need a putty knife to clean the kitchen table after a meal, and that they'd never learn to deposit muddy shoes on the steps before running inside. Okay, we're still working on the muddy shoes, but you understand what I mean—

the laws of time, nature, and children are such that almost nothing can stop growth. We were children once ourselves!

Here are a few of the most-often-published categories of child development:

Ages One to Three

Language plays a key role in your toddler's life. This is the perfect time to introduce picture books that can be shared within her limited attention span. Now mobile, she is anxious to enjoy the full power of movement; walking, climbing, running, and other physical expressions of independence sometimes supersede an interest in "educational" activities. One- to three-year-olds learn through play and interaction. She's beginning to understand symbolic concepts, and she acts that out through make-believe. Also, your toddler is grasping the idea that she can be hurt and may communicate her fears through seemingly unconnected behavior (such as aggression or sleep disturbance).

Pre-Kindergarten Through First Grade

Imagination continues to reign during the years between four and six. Your child may become so engrossed in explorative play that all else is tuned out; you might think he's ignoring you, when in truth he probably didn't hear you. At the same time, he's developing the capacity to reason. Creativity is intense during this age. When creative expression is encouraged without judgment or restriction, these children grow up to be the Dickensons, Edisons, Einsteins, and Picassos of the world. A four- to six-year-old also thinks more deeply; he wants to know how everything works and why it works that way. You may be bombarded with questions day and night—occasionally at inappropriate times. I once had a four-year-old son ask me about women's genitalia in a busy public rest room—*loudly*.

Second Grade Through Early Fifth Grade

Your child's mind is turning to more logical modes of thought. Abstract concepts are playing a larger role in learning. More rational than her younger peers, this is the child who understands that appearances do not always tell the entire (or true) story. She's more empathetic, realizing that the class bully is probably acting more out of fear than bravado. She's also developing a sophisticated sense of humor and loves to tell you jokes. A seven- to ten-year-old may—temporarily—show less interest in creative pursuits. She is much more concerned with *conformity* than individuality; peer relationships take on new significance. Because her aptitude for science, math, and sequential thinking is high, you can encourage creativity in these areas. Puzzles, maps, science kits, question/answer cards, word play, and math games score high marks with this child.

If you've ever been asked, "Why do I have toes?" or "How do birds know when to fly south?" you may want to invest in a series of books by Grolier Publishers. *Questions Kids Ask* is a multi-book set designed to provide children (and their parents) with answers to some of the most common questions of childhood. Look for the books at your local library, or write for information to Grolier Books, 90 Sherman Turnpike, Danbury, CT 06816.

Late Fifth Grade Through Middle School

Adolescents—who range in age from ten to thirteen or fourteen—are struggling with explosive changes in their bodies, interests, relationships, and thought processes. It's the age many parents dread. The word "hormones" can sometimes sound like the word "horrors"—especially if mood swings are making their way through your household. Fortunately, this is also the age of philosophical and ethical development. Preteens are extremely concerned about justice. They're also bounding with creative expression and are better able to communicate their thoughts and feelings. Rebellion is normal and expected; they are beginning to test their wings.

Understanding Different Learning Styles

Think back to your own school days. Did you learn more through books, maps, charts, and visual aides? Could you retain more information from lectures? Perhaps you needed to test the material, feeling your way through learning? No one will fit solidly into a single category, but chances are good that you did better with one mode of learning than with others.

Cynthia Ulrich Tobias, author of *The Way They Learn, The Way We Work,* and *Every Child Can Succeed,* has dedicated her life to understanding and defining learning styles. Every parent can benefit from the information in her books. She identifies, in her book, the following three foundational learning styles:

- **Auditory** learners have the gift of gab. As children, they speak early and incessantly. As adults, they process information verbally, bouncing ideas and problems off anyone willing to listen.

- **Visual** learners need to "see" the picture in order to understand it. As children, they demonstrate artistic ability. As adults, they have an innate capacity for creative expression and interpretation.

- **Kinesthetic** learners are human tornadoes, whirling through life at warp speed. As children, they have a hard time sitting still, preferring action to inactivity. As adults, they're more interested in a "hands on" approach to everything from child rearing to career development.

Those three learning styles comprise the basics, but a house is built on a foundation brick by brick. Through extensive study and research, Tobias has also identified the following substyles:

- **Analytic** learners might easily make up the majority of designers in a puzzle factory. As children, they spend lots of time tinkering with Legos, disassembling toys, and trying to figure out how things work. As adults, they tend to break projects down into manageable steps.
- **Globals** work in the opposite way, grasping what seems like a bunch of unrelated parts and building a whole. These are "big picture" learners. As children, they love to create—be it paintings, poetry, a potted garden, or a playhouse. As adults, they have the ability to communicate complex ideas in a way that's simple and effective.
- **Concrete Sequential** learners are detail-oriented. As children, they excel in math and science. As adults, they form the backbone of office management; they are born problem solvers.
- **Abstract Sequential** thinkers are also concerned with details, but they tend to focus attention on research. As children, they'll pursue interests until they've exhausted all available material. As adults, they're more concerned with reliable facts and statistics than with feelings or hearsay. An abstract sequential thinker wants concrete evidence.

- **Abstract Random** thinkers, on the other hand, rely heavily on the needs and feelings of themselves and others. As children, they try on different roles during make-believe scenarios. As adults, their intuitive understanding of people renders them crucial to harmony at home or work; they smooth ruffled feathers and attend to unmet needs.

- **Concrete Random** thinkers are daring dreamers. As children, they're filled with unlimited ideas, inventing new games or ways of doing things. They often use materials for something other than what they were intended for. As adults, they're the visionaries who refuse to settle for status quo. They're also good motivators and inspirational leaders.

Considering all of those explanations, can you find a combination of styles that best describes your child? Where do you see yourself? Most people fall into three, four, or five of the categories—and you may see elements of yet other styles in their learning. I'd like to introduce you to my own family and give you some examples:

- Bobby is our older son. As an infant he was fascinated with letters and language and could read simple words by the age of two. He talked early and incessantly. Although many of his peers prefer physical outdoor activities, Bobby always chooses playing with Legos over riding his bike. He can entertain himself for hours with quiet pursuits that demand concentration. He's always had, and still has, a very intense personality. He prefers concrete, predictable patterns and schedules; structure is critical to his well-being. Currently, his favorite subject is math. Bobby is an Auditory, Analytic, Concrete Sequential learner with just a smidgen of Abstract Sequential thrown into the mix.

Zachary, our younger son, was a quiet, sensitive, and reserved infant. He began walking at the age of ten months—climbing a flight of stairs the very same day—but didn't talk until he was nearly two. Zachary preferred Playdough (Mattel) or paints over plopping down with a storybook during his early years. He loves to help in the kitchen and now enjoys cookbooks (and other books) with colorful photographs. Zachary memorizes words by sight. He's a master at make-believe, creating elaborate scenarios with his toys. Easygoing, adaptable, and friendly, he's popular on any playground. He wants to be a movie star when he grows up. Zachary is a Visual, Global, Abstract Random learner.

Their father, Steven, works as a project manager in technological development. Although he doesn't always understand *people*, he can dissect the most complex *problem* in amazingly little time. A voracious reader, he is always willing to dig deeper to find the precise information he needs to accomplish a task. He carefully weighs and compares options, never rushing into a decision. At the same time, he's interested in the beauty of the world around him, often stopping to admire a spectacular sunset. Steven is a Visual, Analytic, Abstract Sequential learner.

I'm told I was born with rockets under my feet. Never content to tackle subjects, issues, or problems in a conventional way, I've always insisted on a unique perspective. I did everything early, and I rarely followed directions to the letter; I was and am into shortcuts. Though I can talk the ears off a statue, I need to "experience" something—either personally or vicariously—in order to understand it. At thirty-six, I've discovered that there are more things I'd like to accomplish than there are years in any *two* lifetimes. I'm an Auditory, Kinesthetic, Global, Concrete Random learner.

When you understand your child's learning styles (and your own), it's easier to make sense of school, learning, or family problems. For example:

- An Auditory, Analytic, Concrete Sequential learner will struggle in a classroom filled with quiet games and manipulatives. Also, he may misunderstand a less verbal parent, which might explain why you feel you need to take him step-by-step through a task.
- A Visual, Analytic, Abstract Random learner is certain to be miserable in an environment that includes long periods of lectures. At home, you may—as his parent—wonder why he seems to need you to draw him a picture of a clean, well-organized bedroom.
- A Kinesthetic, Global, Concrete Sequential (or Concrete Random) student might be misdiagnosed as being learning disabled (LD) or as having Attention Deficit Disorder (ADD). The parent of this child might feel overwhelmed with the challenge of preparing her to "fit" into a society that doesn't understand her.

If you'd like to find out more about learning styles—and how they work (or don't work) in the classroom—request additional information from Learning Styles Unlimited, Inc., 1911 SW Campus Drive, Suite 370, Federal Way, WA 98023. If you would like a reproducible profile worksheet, send a self-addressed stamped envelope.

Developing Your Own Games, Activities, and Fun Family Moments

I hope this book has provided you with enough ideas to keep your family entertained for at least a year—maybe longer! I think you'll find that "education" comes in many enjoyable forms. As you've read the chapters, you may have thought of additional activities to enjoy with your children.

No one knows your child better than you do; with an understanding of his developmental level and learning style, you can create fun projects that are ideally suited to his needs and interests. With your encouragement and participation, there will be no stopping him!

I also hope you've reconnected with yourself. Perhaps you've already rediscovered a childhood passion or found a new hobby. Chances are you've started thinking about things you enjoyed in the past. Maybe you've decided to make time in your schedule to enjoy them again!

As a very busy wife, mother, writer, student, friend, and encourager, there have been many days when it's occurred to me that at least some of my stress was due to a lack of *fun* in my life. As my babies grew into boys, I often felt overwhelmed with the added duties of cheerleader, coach, researcher, and information provider (not to mention nose-wiper, personal chef, and chauffeur). I've slowly discovered that I handle my schedule, responsibilities, and even stress more effectively and efficiently when I make the time to *play*. You can, too. Here's how to dream up fun for yourself and your children—and how you can bring education into the process:

Think about the activities you enjoyed as a child. What kinds of games did you like to play? What were your interests? Do you see any connections between your child's interests and your own? Make a list of every subject, type of activity, game, or passion you enjoyed when you were young; include a few of those things you enjoy now. On a separate piece of paper, list the things you most often notice your child doing at play. On a third piece of paper, make a final list that combines your child's preferences with yours, focusing on compatible interests.

364 Ask friends and family members to reminisce about games and play from their school years. What kinds of activities did they enjoy? Why did they find them so enjoyable? Make note of anything that catches your own interest.

365 Reignite your youthful creativity. Chances are it's been a while since you've even thought about finger painting, writing poetry, shaking a tambourine, or pretending to be a superhero. When you were a child, creativity was as natural as breathing; you weren't consciously "creative," you were just a kid having fun. As an adult, you might feel embarrassed to do what was so easy back then. Go to a bookstore or library and look for titles such as:

- *Living Your Life Out Loud*, by Salli Rasberry and Padi S. Elwyn
- *Daring to Be Yourself*, by Alexandra Stoddard
- *Encouraging the Artist in Yourself*, by Sally Warner

Those are my favorites, but any similar books could work. Read one and see where it takes you.

366 We all get plenty of unsolicited catalogs in the mail anyway; why not request a few that will help you get back in touch with your playful side? I've sprinkled the names and addresses of various companies that offer catalogs throughout this book. Some of my personal favorites include *Dick Blick Art Materials* (1-800-447-8192) and *All the Right Stuff* (1-800-799-8697). Browse through catalogs on dreary nights when the children are asleep and television is lousy; you'll be amazed at the ideas you come up with.

367 Subscribe to a few fun, child-focused magazines that regularly publish activities for parents and children alike. You might consider a subscription to a homeschooling magazine; you don't have to be a homeschooling family to subscribe. With just two subscriptions, you can gather several dozen ideas from writers who have done the research for you. I'm particularly fond of *Crayola Kids* and *Family Life* (available wherever magazines are sold); *Cobblestone*, *Calliope*, or *Faces* from Cobblestone Publishing (7 School Street, Petersborough, NH 03458); and *Home Education* magazine (available through Little Professor Booksellers, or get a free copy by e-mail request: HomeEdMag@aol.com). Of that list, only two (*Family Life* and *Home Education* magazine) are geared toward adult readers. Children's magazines are a wonderful resource—and your child will enjoy them, too!

368 One of my favorite ways to jump-start a creative mood is to hop in the van and drive. When I hit the open road—windows rolled down, music cranked up, and city buildings disappearing behind me—I somehow feel lighter. Often I don't have a destination in mind; we explore country areas we're not familiar with. I believe that driving works for me because I have to sit in one place, yet I'm still moving and therefore can think. If you're a kinesthetic or visual learner, go for a drive and ideas will come.

369 When you've gathered ideas, but aren't sure how to work an educational slant into them, ask yourself the following questions and you'll find the scholastic merits of the activity:

- Does this idea involve reading of any kind?
- Does this idea involve writing of any kind?
- Would this activity involve any life science (botany, biology, zoology, ecology, etc.)? Does it involve any physical science (geology, chemistry, physics, etc.)?
- Are there any possible elements of mathematics involved?
- Could we look into the history of something related to this activity?
- Could we tie in how children in other countries might do something similar to this activity?
- What personal qualities could be developed through this activity (cooperation, empathy, patience, self-esteem, etc.)?
- Does this activity fit my child's learning styles, or will I need to adapt it slightly?
- Is this activity age-appropriate for my child? Does she have the development necessary to enjoy it? If not, could an older child or adult help her?

The Legacy of Living, Loving, and Learning Together Will Span Generations

The true test of fun family learning is the memory it leaves behind. When your children associate learning with warm feelings of time spent together—reading, playing, laughing, sharing, exploring, creating, experiencing all that is around us—they gain more than a lifelong interest in education. The memories of each priceless moment will carry them through the twists and turns of this roller-coaster existence we call life. One shared activity builds on another, and another, and another, until your children walk into their adult lives with the confidence that they're prepared for all that lies ahead.

> *"Light tomorrow with today!"*
>
> —ELIZABETH BARRETT BROWNING

This book hasn't just been about creative learning, it's been about *family—your* family, *your* memories, *your* children. This book has detailed 369 ways for you to make memories together, to *relax*, and to *enjoy* each other. Woven into every page is the message that, no matter what your circumstances, regardless of "conventional" wisdom—and casting aside all doubts—*there is limitless potential for accomplishment and success residing in your home*. It's a legacy that you can pass on to your children, who will share the magic with their own children.

It may be hard to believe that something as simple as incorporating a little play into your daily routine can have such an enormous impact, but it can and will. There will still be harried days, long nights, and sibling arguments, yet overall you'll notice improvement. Your children will, too. Years from now, they may not remember whether the house was always clean or the laundry was always done. It won't matter much to them whether you nailed your assignments or landed a big promotion. When they look back, they'll remember happy times spent with you; they'll remember that you believed in their abilities and made time to play.

No one can put a price tag on that . . . and it's as easy as reading a book, baking cookies, or having a child beat your pants off in a card game.

Resources

The information in this book is the product of more than ten years of voracious reading, the shared tips of friends and family, and adapted ideas from Internet resources and forums. I have not, to the best of my knowledge, directly quoted any sources other than those that are noted within the text. However, I thought it might be useful to provide you with a list of books, magazines, and other resources that I've found to be invaluable.

Books

Look for these new and classic titles in libraries or at a resale (used) bookstore:

- *The Art of the Possible*, by Alexandra Stoddard (Morrow, 1995); most of the concepts can be applied to parenting as well
- *Art Projects Around the Calendar*, by Robert Henkes (J. Weston Walch, 1991)
- *Beginning Science*, by Dr. Jerome J. Notkin (Grosset & Dunlap, 1970)
- *Born Dancing*, by Evelyn Thoman and Sue Browder (Harper, 1987)
- *Breakthrough Parenting*, by John Maxwell (Focus on the Family, 1996)
- *Daring to Be Yourself*, by Alexandra Stoddard (Avon, 1992)

- *Encouraging the Artist in Yourself*, by Sally Warner (St. Martin's Press, 1996)
- *Ending the Homework Hassle*, by John Rosemond (Andrews & McMeel, 1990)
- *The Essential Guide to Nature Walking in the United States*, by Charles Cook (Henry Holt and Co., 1996)
- *Every Child Can Succeed*, by Cynthia Ulrich Tobias (Focus on the Family, 1996)
- *Everyday Pediatrics for Parents*, by Elmer Grossman, M.D. (Celestial Arts, 1996); includes valuable information about family life, childhood development, and common concerns
- *Help for Hurting Moms*, by Kathy Collard Miller (Evergreen Communications, Inc., 1990)
- *Homework Without Tears*, by Lee Canter and Lee Hausner, Ph.D. (Lee Canter & Associates, 1987)
- *How Children Learn*, by John Holt (Addison-Wesley, rev. ed. 1995)
- *How to Help Your Child with Homework*, by Marguerite Radencich and Jeanne S. Schumm (Free Spirit Publishing, rev. ed. 1996)
- *The Hurried Child*, by David Elkind (Addison-Wesley, 1988); if you're running harder just to stay in place, this book is a must!
- *Improving Your Child's Schoolwork*, by Lawrence Greene (Prima Publishing, 1995)
- *The Inner World of Childhood*, by Frances Wickes (Weiser, 1966); a delightful older book that's worth searching for

- *In Their Own Way*, by Thomas Armstrong, Ph.D. (Jeremy P. Tarcher, 1988)
- *Learning All The Time*, by John Holt (Addison-Wesley, 1990)
- *Let Prayer Change Your Life*, by Becky Tiribassi (Nelson, 1995)
- *Liberated Parents, Liberated Children*, by Adele Faber and Elaine Mazlish (Avon, 1976)
- *Living Your Life Out Loud*, by Salli Rasberry and Padi S. Elwyn (Pocket Books, 1995); if this book doesn't help you get in touch with your inner child, nothing will
- *Making Children Mind Without Losing Yours*, by Dr. Kevin Leman, Psychologist (Revell, 1983)
- *100 Flowers and How They Got Their Names*, by Diana Wells (Algonquin Books of Chapel Hill, 1997)
- *Playhouses You Can Build*, by David and Jeanie Stiles (Chapters Publishing, Inc., 1993)
- *The Prayer Partner Notebook*, by Becky Tiribassi (Oliver-Nelson, 1990)
- *The Radiant Child*, by Thomas Armstrong, Ph.D. (Theosophical Publishing House, 1985)
- *Raising a Son*, by Don Elium (Ten Speed Press, 1992)
- *Raising a Thinking Child*, by Myrna B. Shure, Ph.D. (Henry Holt, 1994)
- *Raising Self-Reliant Children in a Self-Indulgent World*, by H. Stephen Glenn and Jane Nelsen (Prima Publishing, 1988)

- *Self-Esteem: A Family Affair*, by Jean Illsey Clarke (Harper, 1985); a classic that belongs in every family library
- *Still Teaching Ourselves*, by Agnes Leistico (Home Education Press, 1995)
- *The Way They Learn*, by Cynthia Ulrich Tobias (Focus on the Family, 1994)
- *The Way We Work*, by Cynthia Ulrich Tobias (Focus on the Family, 1995)

HOME BUSINESS

- *How to Open and Operate a Home-Based Crafts Business*, by Kenn Oberrecht (Globe Pequot, 1994)
- *Marketing Without Advertising*, by Michael Phillips and Salli Rasberry (Nolo Press, 1996)
- *The Self-Publishing Manual*, by Dan Poynter (Para Publishing, 1996)
- *Self-Publish Your Own Picture Book*, by Howard Gregory (H. Gregory, 1989)

Magazines

- *Better Homes and Gardens*, P.O. Box 55220, Boulder, CO 80323
- *Child: The Essential Guide for Today's Parents*, P.O. Box 3175, Harlan, IA 51593
-  *Country Living Gardener*, P.O. Box 7475, Red Oak, IA 51591

- *Family Circle*, P.O. Box 5204, Harlan, IA 51593
- *Family Fun*, P.O. Box 37032, Boone, IA 50037
- *Family Life*, P.O. Box 52220, Boulder, CO 80322
- *Home Education*, P.O. Box 1083, Tonasket, WA 98855
- *Parenting Magazine*, P.O. Box 56861, Boulder, CO 80328
- *Working Mother*, P.O. Box 5240, Harlan, IA 51593

Organizations

- **Alliance for Parental Involvement in Education:** P.O. Box 59, East Chatham, NY 12060
- **Association for Childhood Education International:** 11501 Georgia Avenue, Suite 315, Wheaton, MD 20902; 1-800-423-3563
- **At-Home Dads:** 61 Brightwood Avenue, North Andover, MA 01845
- **Families and Work Institute:** 330 Seventh Avenue, New York, NY 10001
- **Formerly Employed Mothers At The Leading Edge (FEMALE):** P.O. Box 31, Elmhurst, IL 60126
- **Home School Legal Defense Association:** P.O. Box 159, Paeonian Springs, VA 20129
- **National Association for the Education of Young Children:** 1509 Sixteenth Street NW, Washington, DC 20036
- **National Association of Partners in Education:** 901 N. Pitt Street, Suite 320, Alexandria, VA 22314

Special Needs

- **Adoptive Families of America:** 1-800-372-3300
- **National Committee to Prevent Child Abuse:** 1-800-244-5373
- **Parents Without Partners:** 1-800-637-7974
- **Stepfamily Association of America:** 1-800-735-0329

Internet Resources

Through America Online

- *American Demographics* Web site and database access
- *American History* subscription service and database access
- Home Office or Writers' forums
- *National Geographic* Web site and database access
- Rand McNally database access
- *Scientific American* subscription and database access
- Smithsonian Web site, membership services, and database access
- *Woman's Day* database access and interactive forum
- Homeschool interactive forum
- Parenting interactive forum

Through CompuServe

- *Books in Print* (power search on title, author, or subject)

- Magazine Database Plus (power search on publication, date, subject, or key words)
- Time-Warner Lifestyles interactive forum
- *Women's Wire* interactive forum
- *Working from Home* interactive forum

Index

H

Y

Z

Disneyland® & Southern California with Kids, 1998–1999

Carey Simon

U.S. $14.00
Can. $18.95
ISBN: 0-7615-1242-X
paperback / 272 pages

Disneyland & Southern California with Kids is an essential guide to "kid-proofing" a visit to Southern California's many attractions. Not simply a guide to Disneyland, this book offers advice for parents and children headed to Knott's Berry Farm, Universal Studios, Magic Mountain, the San Diego Zoo, and many other Southland attractions. Also included are tips on finding restaurants and hotels with "kid appeal," ways to save money on the Disneyland trip, plus parades, fireworks, and special shows that first-timers frequently miss.

To order, call (800) 632-8676 or visit us online at www.primapublishing.com

To Order Books

Please send me the following items:

Quantity	Title	Unit Price	Total
______	Walt Disney World with Kids, 1998	$ 14.00	$ ______
______	Disneyland and Southern California...	$ 14.00	$ ______
______	______	$ ______	$ ______
______	______	$ ______	$ ______
______		$	$ ______

*Shipping and Handling depend on Subtotal.

Subtotal	Shipping/Handling
$0.00–$14.99	$3.00
$15.00–$29.99	$4.00
$30.00–$49.99	$6.00
$50.00–$99.99	$10.00
$100.00–$199.99	$13.50
$200.00+	Call for Quote

Foreign and all Priority Request orders:
Call Order Entry department
for price quote at 916-632-4400

This chart represents the total retail price of books only (before applicable discounts are taken).

Subtotal	$ ______
Deduct 10% when ordering 3–5 books	$ ______
7.25% Sales Tax (CA only)	$ ______
8.25% Sales Tax (TN only)	$ ______
5.0% Sales Tax (MD and IN only)	$ ______
7.0% G.S.T. Tax (Canada only)	$ ______
Shipping and Handling*	$ ______
Total Order	$ ______

By Telephone: With American Express, MC, or Visa,
call 800-632-8676 or 916-632-4400. Mon–Fri, 8:30-4:30.

WWW: http://www.primapublishing.com

By Internet E-mail: sales@primapub.com

By Mail: Just fill out the information below and send with your remittance to:

Prima Publishing
P.O. Box 1260BK
Rocklin, CA 95677

Name ______________________

Address ______________________

City ______________ State ______ ZIP ______

American Express/MC/Visa# ______________ Exp. ______

Check/money order enclosed for $ ______________ Payable to Prima Publishing

Daytime telephone ______________________

Signature ______________________